MW00397137

FORGOTTEN HEROES

The story of two forgotten World War I Medal of Honor heroes from the only county in the United States to produce two Medal of Honor recipients in that war.

by Jim Claborn

With Danny Underwood and Michael Lee "Mike" Beck

Copyright 2017

ISBN-13:978-1539651246

ISBN-10:123965124X

FOREWORD

When 110-year-old Frank Buckles died in 2011, the last living veteran of World War I died, too. Only a tiny few of the oldest folks have the faintest memory of having lived during that war. But, the rest of us don't. In that war, soldiers were actually gassed and did go "over the top" in deadly 18th Century "light brigade-type" charges into the face of 20th Century weapons like tanks, airplanes and machineguns. They performed unbelievable acts of bravery and inhuman and terrible slaughter was the result.

Jimmy Claborn's newest book, FORGOTTEN HEROES celebrates the centennial of the United States entry into that war, the 100th Anniversary, with a story of two different and unlikely, little known heroes from his own neighborhood in 'Davy Crockett Country,' Morristown, Tennessee.

During World War I the Medal of Honor, the nation's highest award for valor, would be awarded 119 times. Thirty-three went to soldiers who died earning them, while 86 men lived to receive the award. There are 3,144 counties or their equivalents in the U.S. There are 95 counties in Tennessee. Along with being home to Davy Crockett, Sam Houston and Sergeant York, Tennessee is also home to seven World War I Medal of Honor recipients.

Claborn's home county, tiny little Hamblen County, in upper East Tennessee is the only county in America to be counted as the home of two World War I Medal of Honor recipients, Sergeant

Edward Talley and Private Calvin Ward, whose stories and lives are featured in *FORGOTTEN HEROES*.

While Sergeant York would become the nation's hero, both Talley (who died in 1950) and Ward (who killed himself in 1967) would, tragically, be forgotten. Why and how? One would become fairly successful while the other became a wanderer, suffering from PTSD, which, then, few knew anything about. Remember, Post-Traumatic Stress Syndrome was unknown at the time though both men, especially Ward, would suffer from it.

This book is an important contribution. Jimmy's personal and heartfelt style gives life and breath and a sense of "place" to a gripping tale of heroism and valor. You'll see, in time, that this book will become extremely well known and popular, an important documentary. Jimmy Claborn is unique to his place. It's his home. He knows it loves it, and the people in it. Because it's his life's work, he is able to share this book with us, remarkably. I highly recommend it. *FORGOTTEN HEROES* is a heartfelt, personal and gripping tale.

Bill Landry, author and host of TV's *Heartlands Series*.

ACKNOWLEDGEMENT

Much of the credit for this book should be shared with two friends, Danny Underwood and Michael Lee "Mike" Beck.

More than a decade has passed since statewide military historian Mike Beck called with an opportunity to visit with Calvin Ward's last surviving sibling. Maxine Meade would give us a personal view of her brother that would reveal much more about Ward than would any written word. Mike and I would also visit with Calvin's niece, Cleo Sipe Purkey, who was close to her uncle, and she would provide us with many photos and personal memories. Historian Donahue Bible would take us to Calvin's birthplace, which would give a good measurement of the hero's beginnings.

Mary Alice Harville would spend a number of her early years with her Aunt Mattie and "Uncle Ed" Talley and would share many memories, as well as photos and documents of the old hero. In addition, Mike and I would take a Virginia trip that would include VFW historian Doyle Smith, Paul Murr and Edward Talley's great nephew Judge Eddie Beckner. Judge Beckner had spent his early years with Ed and Mattie Talley at the Talley home in Appalachia, Virginia.

Just prior to the shut-off date for this publication, Mike would also arrange a visit with another Talley nephew, Bill Moore. Through their memories and photos, Bill, along with Mary Alice, Judge Beckner, Cleo Sipe and Maxine Meade would prove to be the seed for the growth of this book and would allow us to see their kinspersons as they were in life.

Soon after the book was started, Danny Underwood would come on board to use his skills as a retired Naval Intelligence veteran. Danny would dust off his research talents and would spend many months of digging up remarkable photographs and almost forgotten details of the two heroes and their times. Much more than was locally known about both Talley and Ward was learned as the result of Danny's efforts and much of the credit for this book is due to his long and hard work.

VFW historian Doyle Smith would also prove most valuable in gathering military-related details. Ginger Burchett of the Jefferson County Standard Banner would graciously offer to share her knowledge of the mechanics of producing a book. Betty Martin is a well-known across the area as an expert genealogist and is an author with a number of books. She would prove invaluable in sharing her publishing experience and in her intensive help toward the birth of this book.

State Senator Steve Southerland has a deep love for Hamblen County, his home county, and would help us through doors that would otherwise require much more time and effort on our part. Several other dear friends were also a great help and would be quick to assist and offer encouragement to this author who is quick to admit he has limited writing skills.

My wife, Robin, daughter Dana Tara and son-in-law Brian Papworth were supportive of my spending months looking at a keyboard that could have otherwise have been put toward other needed chores. Other special friends would also add encouragement in the times that I would find my other responsibilities almost making this project impossible to complete. As a team we've tried very hard to do a good job on this book, but while no historian can be completely accurate, this book will have some mistakes. Please forgive those mistakes and just know that we did our best.

Lastly, I would like to thank my God for giving me this opportunity, as well as the blessing for having lived in the best country known in the history of Mankind.

Jim Claborn

FORGOTTEN HEROES

The story of two forgotten World War I Medal of Honor heroes from the only county in the United States to produce two Medal of Honor recipients in that war.

CONTENTS

FOREWORD by Bill Landry

Chapter One

THE CONGRESSIONAL MEDAL OF HONOR

Sergeant Edward R. Talley's Medal of Honor

From the time of the Civil War, the Medal of Honor has been America's highest award for valor in action against an enemy force which can be bestowed upon an individual serving in the armed services of the United States of America. With so many soldiers of the Civil War receiving the Medal of Honor, a stricter evaluation of criteria and policies regarding the medal began a period of rigid formulation. Receiving the Medal today represents a most monumental achievement. It is entirely possible, however, that those same requirements might well have resulted in many service members being missed entirely who deserved the recognition, but whose recommendations were entangled in the lengthy process.

As of this writing, 3,494 Medals of Honor have been awarded with almost half of those having gone to Civil War soldiers. In its history, 621 Medals have been presented posthumously. Currently, there are 80 living Medal of Honor recipients and those heroes should be considered as America's rarest gems. During America's 1917-1918 involvement in World War I, 119 servicemen would receive the Medal of Honor, of which seven would be Tennesseans. Thirty-three of those medals would be presented posthumously, with 86 going to then still-living recipients.

The 50 states of the United States are divided into 3,144 counties and their equivalents. Tennessee has 95 of those counties. Hamblen County, Tennessee, is the state's third smallest and is the United States' only county to have had two World War I Medal of Honor recipients who would list their home of record as tiny Hamblen County. Those two recipients were Sergeant Edward Talley and Private Calvin Ward who both likely were among the highest decorated American soldiers of the war. Sergeant Alvin C. York unquestionably earned his award and would receive national recognition, while Talley and Ward have both been virtually forgotten within their own community.

While Talley was a native of Hamblen County's Russellville, Ward was born on the southern tip of nearby Greene County and would move to Morristown as a youngster. Upon entering the

Army, he would list his home address as West First North Street in Morristown, and would spend his later years in the town. Available information tells us that both men lightly knew each other before entering the service, and were only a few miles apart when they earned their Medals of Honor, Talley on October 7, 1918 and Ward on October 8, 1918.

On October 7, the then 28 year-old Sergeant Edward Talley was near Poncheux, France when he witnessed his comrades being ripped apart by enemy machine gun fire. Having had enough, he grabbed his bolt-action rifle and charged into the machine gun fire. He succeeded in killing or wounding six of the enemy and putting the gun out of action. His continuous fire would keep the enemy from bringing up a second gun. Sergeant Edward Talley would earn the Medal of Honor on October 7, 1918 by single-handedly charging and destroying an enemy machine gun nest, and would prevent a second gun from being set up.

Sergeant Edward Robert Talley

Russellville's Medal of Honor recipient Sergeant Edward R. Talley. (Bill Moore)

Talley's Medal of Honor citation would read as follows:

"From the Adjutant General, A.E.F. to Commanding General, 30th Division

Subject 'Decorations'

The President in the name of Congress, under the date of April 2nd, 1919, has awarded the Medal of Honor to the following named soldier for an act of conspicuous gallantry and intrepidity set forth after his name Sergeant Edward R. Talley, Co. L, 117th Infantry (1309598)

Undeterred by seeing several comrades killed in action in attempting to put a hostile machine gun nest out of action, Sergeant Talley attacked the position single-handed. Armed only with a rifle, he rushed the nest in the face of intense enemy fire, killed or wounded at least six of the crew and silenced the gun. When the enemy attempted to bring forth another gun and ammunition, Sergeant Talley drove them back by effective fire from his rifle.

The Adjutant General of the Army has been requested to make the presentation to Sergeant Talley.

By command of General Pershing – signed F.L. Whitley, Adjutant General, Hq. 30th Division, Camp Jackson S.C. April 28th, 1919."

The citation was further signed on November 25, 1924, by John K. Kerr, Secretary of War.

In addition to the Medal of Honor, Talley would also receive a number of foreign decorations that would include the French Croix de Guerre with Palm, the Belgium Croix de Guerre with Silver Star, the Portuguese War Cross of the Third Class, the British Distinguished Conduct Metal, the Italian Cross of Military Valor, the French Medaille Militaire and the Montenegrin Military Medal.

Private Calvin John Ward

Calvin Ward was born on the southern edge of Greene County, but would soon move to Morristown. On October 8, 1918, and one day after Talley's heroism, just-turned 19 years-old Calvin was in a muddy foxhole near Estrees, France with the remnant of his unit, where they were being ravaged by an enemy machine gun. "I was rottening and I'd had enough," he would later tell Eddie Shipley, who was then working at a downtown Morristown lunch counter. Ward, and Knoxville's Sergeant Buck Karnes, had both had all they could take. Fixing bayonets on their British bolt action rifles, they charged into the blazing machine gun, killing three and capturing seven of the enemy. Karnes would also receive the Medal of Honor for this action.

Calvin Ward would spend his early and later years in Morristown. He would be presented with the Medal of Honor in France by General John J. Pershing. (National Archives}

Calvin Ward's Medal of Honor citation would read as follows:

"The Adjutant General, American E. F.

Commanding General, 30th Division.

Decorations.

1.   The President, in the name of Congress, under the date of 11 January 1919, has awarded the Medal of Honor to Private Calvin John Ward, (AS No. 1507698), Company D, 117th Infantry, for the following act of conspicuous gallantry and intrepidity:

For conspicuous gallantry and intrepidity, above and beyond the call of duty, in action with the enemy, near Estrees, France, 8 October 1918.

During and (sic) advance, PVT Ward's company was held up by a machine gun, which was enfilading the line. Accompanied by a non-commissioned officer, he advanced against this post and succeeded in reducing the nest and killing three and capturing seven of the enemy and their guns."

Next of Kin: Mrs. Laura Ward, Mother, 749 1st North St., Morristown, Tenn.

2. The Commander-in-Chief, will personally make presentation of the Medal of Honor and you will be informed later as to the time and place of presentation.

3. It is directed that you inform these headquarters, by wire, as to the present location of Private Ward.

      By Command of General Pershing
      J.A. ULIO
      Adjutant General."

In addition to the Medal of Honor, Ward would also receive the World War I Victory Medal and Army of Occupation World War, as well as the British Distinguished Conduct Medal, French Croix de Guerre with Palm, French Foreign Legion medal, French Medalle Militare, Italian Croix de Guerre, Portuguese War Cross (Cruz de Guerre), and the Montenegrin Medalle Por La Bravoure Militaire.

Chapter Two

AMERICA IN WORLD WAR I

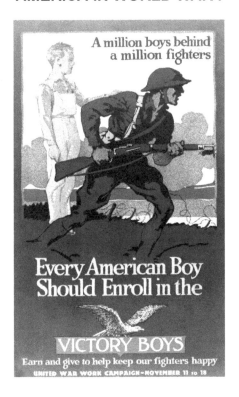

With the passing of 110 year-old Frank Buckles in 2011, America would lose its last-living veteran of World War I, 93 years after his struggle. Earl Horner of Hamblen County,

Tennessee's neighboring Jefferson County had died a decade earlier and would be one of that area's last surviving World War I combat soldiers. Horner would recall his unit being placed inside a barbed wire fence upon their arrival in France to keep them from the French girls who had lost so many of their own men. He would tell of airplanes overhead with pilots sometimes shooting at each other with pistols and of clumsy tanks that would hardly move faster than a man could walk.

Earl Horner (r.) of Jefferson County would become one of the last of the area's World War I combat veterans. (Jack Nichols)

In early 1917 Americans were still talking about the hanging of Mary the elephant which had occurred a year earlier in Erwin, Tennessee. A new car could be had for $500 and bread was seven cents a loaf. Buffalo Bill Cody would die, but Dizzy Gillespie and John F. Kennedy would be born. Former pro baseball player Billy Sunday was the country's most influential evangelist and the first Moon Pie was produced in Chattanooga. "Over There" and "It's a Long Way to Tipperary" would become popular patriotic songs by the end of the year. Woodrow Wilson, whose slogan was that he would "keep us out of war", would begin his second term as President of the United States and America would enter the World War I on Friday, April 6, 1917, shortly after Wilson would begin his second term.

Main Street, Morristown, Tennessee (c.1920). Booming during the World War I era, Morristown was the county seat and largest town in Hamblen County, Tennessee. At the time, the entire population of the county was 21,800 residents. (Rose Center)

Sixteen trains were passing through Morristown daily in the early months of 1917 as town folk were anticipating the Easter holiday. The Lynn Sheely Company was offering the latest Victor recordings while the Roberts and Turner Drug Store advertised 'DDD Tonic' which would wash away skin sores and Cardui Tonic, which questioned: "Are You Worn Out?" Pangle-Cobble clothing store was offering three pairs of men's socks for 25 cents and men's indigo overalls for $1.00. A vest pocket Kodak camera could be had at The Corner Drug Store for $6.00 while the Weesner-Reams store was selling oil cook stoves for $12.75. The Chero-Cola company was opening and Jason P. Graves (who would become the town's last-living Civil War veteran) was contracting for painting and decorating work. Dosser Brothers was selling men's oxfords for $3.50 and women's low-cuts for $2.50. The Princess Theater was showing 'The Unborn' – admission 15 cents, while the Strand Theater would be showing 'Birth of a Nation' beginning June 4th.

World War I, one of history's deadliest conflicts with 70 million people being mobilized, would produce 37 million military and civilian casualties, of which 26 million would be killed. The war had its formal beginning on July 28, 1914, when Austria-Hungary declared war on Serbia. Other countries quickly became involved with the two main groups of antagonists joining either the Allied Forces or the Central Powers. Drawing in the world's greatest powers, the war would be fought with 20th Century technology, but with 19th Century tactics, at an absurd cost of human lives with generals in their cushy headquarters directing their men into massive slaughters.

While battles occurred in many different parts of the world, the most massive groups of combatants would battle in Belgium and France. By the later part of September, 1914, the Battle of the Marne, which was fought just north of Paris, had placed the war into a stalemate, leaving the two sides facing each other from long lines of opposing trenches often separated by 50' deep barriers of barbed wire.

That situation would become brutal with the most common way of taking an enemy trench being to go "Over the Top" across "No Man's Land" where very often many of the attackers would be slaughtered by machinegun and artillery fire, aerial bombardment, or poisonous gas. At the Battle the Somme in July 1916, the British Expeditionary Force led by Sir Douglas Haig would suffer 60,000 killed in just one day of fighting. By 1917 so many men had been killed that the war became a war of attrition where, by the end of the war on November 11, 1918, nine million soldiers and 17 million civilians would be dead. To add to the mortality an influenza epidemic during the same era would kill three times as many as would be killed in the war.

The mood in the United States had been to stay out of the war but the sinking of American ships by German U-boats, as well as an attempt by Germany to ally with Mexico, would be the main factors in bringing America into the war in 1917. In that same year Russia would leave the war. Prior to America's entry into the conflict, a good number of Americans were already involved in the fighting. Those Americans would include brothers Kiffen and Paul Rockwell of Newport, Tennessee, who had already joined the earlier Americans in the fight "Over There." Kiffen would become the first American pilot to shoot down an enemy plane.

With America having been caught with a small standing army of 158,800 regular and 67,000 National Guard soldiers and a small navy, a draft was enacted that would bring 2.8 million men between ages 18 and 40 into the military. A majority of those men would go overseas where 1,390,000 would see combat, with 293,000 of those becoming casualties of some sort. One-fourth of those soldiers would arrive in Europe during the first year of American's participation while three-fourths would arrive during the last six months of the conflict, with 300,000 of those soldiers arriving in the month of July, 1918. With America's typical combat unit being a division of about 1,000 officers and 27,000 men, 42 of those divisions would be sent to France.

Along with the massive commitment of troops, the U.S., then with a population of 103 million, would become a massive logistical powerhouse. Beginning with the American involvement France would see American-build roads, railroads, ports, hospitals, barracks, and even a huge ice house with a capacity for 500 tons daily. A cold storage facility would also be built with a capacity for the beef from 26,000 head of cattle.

With so many men flooding into the military and without having adequate planning for such a situation, the training for those men was haphazard at the best, sometimes with the trainees given pieces of wood to be carved into "training rifles". Britain and France would send nearly 800 officers and non-commissioned officers with experience in the newer trench warfare system to help in the training camps. This would prove valuable, as most new American soldiers had little idea of the type of war they were to fight.

After arriving in France, many soldiers would receive more training by the Allies before leaving for the line. With America not being able to provide enough standard weapons for their soldiers, many would be issued British Enfields, while many machine gunners would get the horrible French Chauchet light machine gun – said by many to be "the worst machine gun ever manufactured". For heavier machine guns, they were often given the slow-firing French Hotchkiss, which required a team of mules to be put in place.

The first regular American casualties would occur on September 4, 1917. American engineer units would see action at Cambrio in November, 1917, and again in March, 1918. By the summer of 1918, one million American soldiers under General John J. Pershing had arrived in France and 10,000 would continue arriving daily until the end of the war. The British and French wanted to use the Americans as fill-ins to replace their casualties but Pershing wanted to keep his army together. However, to appease the Allies he would provide two of his divisions to be under their control. From his headquarters in Paris, Pershing would direct that "only officers full of mental and physical vigor should be sent here".

Prior to the arrival of the Americans the Allies were expecting a bunch of un-disciplined and inexperienced soldiers. In time the newcomers would prove how wrong that evaluation was. By October, 1918 the American divisions would be holding 101 miles of the battle line, or 23 percent of the entire western front. While

100,000 Union soldiers would fight the Civil War Battle of Gettysburg, 550,000 Americans would be involved in the Battle of St. Mihel. One million shells would be fired at St. Mihel in just four hours, which would be the highest concentration of artillery fire in recorded history. Around 1,200,000 Americans would take part in the 47 days of the Meuse-Argonne Battle.

Much of the war would be spent in wet and miserable trenches where cold, rain, knee-high mud, terrible toilet options, trench foot and various outer maladies, and "pants rabbits" (lice) would become an everyday fare. The mixing together of so many people would also rapidly spread diseases to those who had never developed immunities and the artillery fire, gas attacks, aerial bombardments, machinegun fire, and charges across "No Man's Land" would produce so many dead bodies that many times they couldn't be buried for weeks at a time. For every man killed in battle, six would be wounded, with five of those six being returned to duty after they had begun to heal.

The command "Over the Top!" would find men running across No Man's Land, mud, shell holes and masses of barbed wire in nearly suicidal 19th Century mass attacks into the murderous fire of 20th Century weapons. The war was a human meat grinder, with many American infantry companies suffering an 80 percent casualty rate of their original complement. Fighting alongside British, French and Australian units would often find the "doughboys" using foreign and unfamiliar weapons and eating the food of the other Allies, which wasn't of the quantity necessary for the larger Americans or of a taste to their liking. Most of the young American soldiers were far from home for the first time and were often uneducated. Their year of war would affect them for their remaining lifetime.

The war was particularly costly for the Americans that were under foreign Allied commanders who would often commit their troops in full-frontal attacks, a disastrous tactic which had already been questioned by General Pershing, particularly after his earlier expedition in Mexico. First thought to be untrained and undisciplined by the other Allies, the fresher and hard-fighting Americans were soon welcomed by the exhausted Allies. They would play a significant role in ending the war which would come on "11-11-11", the 11th hour of the 11th day of the 11th month, when the Armistice to end the war would be signed in a railroad car at Campiegne, France.

References:

Pershing, John J., Headquarters A.E.F., Paris. "Officers of Full Mental and Physical Vigor Required", July 28, 1917.

Transportation and Logistics, International Encyclopedia of the First World War (WW1).

Chapter Three

THE THIRTIETH INFANTRY DIVISION

The two World War I Medal of Honor recipients who would count Hamblen County, Tennessee, as their home, Sergeant Edward R. Talley and Private Calvin John Ward, were both members of the 117th Infantry Regiment of the 30th Infantry Division. Talley, of Company L, would earn his medal on October 7, 1918, near Poncheux, France while Ward, of Company D, would earn the award the next day near Estrees, France. This is the story of that division up to and through that war.

During World War I an American division would consist of about 1,000 officers and 27,000 men, with those divisions being roughly twice the size of those of other countries involved in the war. A British division would number about 15,000 men each while French and German divisions would contain about 12,000. During the war the Army had plans calling for 80 divisions being trained and overseas before July, 1919, with the number reaching 100 by the end of the war, which was a huge endeavor for the U.S.'s then population of 103 million. Fortunately, the war would end on November 11, 1918, after 42 divisions had been sent to France. Also sent along were a large number of support troops, as well as artillery.

Of those 42 divisions sent to France, 29 would see active combat service, while the others would be used as replacements, or would arrive late in the war. Of those 42 divisions, seven would be Regular Army divisions, 11 would be organized from the National Guard, and 11 would be made up of National Army troops. The 30th Infantry Division, nicknamed "The Old Hickory Division" after President Andrew Jackson, would be one of those National Guard units. At a time when the National Guard was considered an undisciplined and undertrained military branch, the war would see the 30th emerge as one of the most hard-fighting and highly decorated American units of the war.

The beginnings of the proud heritage of the 30th can be traced to before the Revolutionary War when local militia units in what is now East Tennessee were formed to protect the settlements from Creek and Cherokee Indian raids. During the Revolutionary War Colonel John Sevier would bring together militia units from along the Holston and Nolichucky River country to form the Militia Company of East Tennessee. That company would join with other "Over-Mountain Men" to defeat a superior British force at the Battle of King's Mountain in South Carolina on October 7, 1780.

Volunteer Tennessee militias from would fight in the War of 1812, the Mexican-American War and the Civil War. On March 25, 1887 Tennessee militia units would be absorbed into the National Guard of the United States, with the newly-formed Third Tennessee Infantry Regiment being headquartered in Knoxville. Deployed for the Spanish- American War in 1898, the Third would be mustered out of federal service in 1899. Soon reorganized in Knoxville, it would become the Sixth Infantry Regiment until it was re-designated once again as the Third Infantry Regiment in 1903.

Called to the Mexican Punitive Expedition to pursue Francisco "Pancho" Villa on July 3, 1916, the Third would see service along the Mexican border. After returning home, they would be mustered out of federal service on March 14, 1917, only to be called back to federal service several weeks later. The old Third would soon be designated as the 117th Infantry Regiment of the 59th Brigade of the 30th Infantry Division and ordered to report to Camp Sevier, near Greenville, South Carolina.

At the time, Camp Sevier was mostly a pine forest where the earlier arriving soldiers would be tasked with cutting trees to clear and build much of their camp, as well as performing close order drill. This hard physical activity would aid in hardening and strengthen the men in a manner that would later be much to their advantage. On July 18, 1917, National Guard units from North and South Carolina and Tennessee had been combined and would gain the new designation as the 30th Infantry Division of the National Guard under the command of Major General Edward M. Lewis. During that August and September troops from Camp Gordon, Georgia, would also be transferred to the 30th. Also added to their numbers were troops from Camps Jason and Pike, most of whom were from the Midwestern states.

Organization of the Division would include the 59th Infantry Brigade, which was made of the 117th and 118th Infantry Regiments and the 114th Machine Gun Battalion. Also included was the 60th Infantry Brigade which included the 119th and 120th Infantry Regiments and the 115th Machine Gun Battalion. Other divisional troops would include the 105th Engineers, 113th Machine Gun Battalion, 105th Field Signal Battalion, 105th Military Police, 105th Ammunition Train, 105th Supply Train, 105th

Engineer Train, 105th Sanitary Train, three artillery regiments, Ambulance units, field hospitals and the Headquarters unit.

The division would officially get the nickname "The Old Hickory Division" on March 26, 1918. As it was still developing the Division would begin training in mid-September, which would last until the end of April, 1918. On May 2, 1918, the Division's headquarters (DHQ) and the infantry organizations would board trains and leave Camp Sevier for Camp Mills, Long Island, New York. Other units would be sent to Camp Merritt, near Cresskill, New Jersey. Beginning May 11th and lasting through the 19th, the Division Headquarters (DHQ) and infantry would sail from New York and Hoboken and would arrive in England on May 24th. By June 5th other sections had arrived in England, where after several days of travel and rest, the Infantry would depart for Calais and the artillery for LaHarve, France. Once in France, the 30th would arrive near St. Omer, to be billeted in the British Second Army's Eperlocques Training Area.

In 1936, Elmer A. Murphy, a former member of the Medical Corps, would tell about the ocean crossing in his book, "The 30th Division In The World War."

"As the ships that transported the 30th Division were of several registries, British dominating, the rations issued the men were their first taste of foreign fare. Tea, mutton, goat meat, orange marmalade, hardtack and other strange articles of food caused first bewilderment, then hunger and finally loud protests from boys accustomed to beans, potatoes, bacon and assorted stews and who had at home been accustomed to pork chops, fried chicken, gravy, hot biscuits and pie. The ships larders must have been over-stocked with mutton, for it was served at least once and often twice every day. Then there was the superfluvity (sic) of orange marmalade, an evil-tasting mixture that evidently delights the British palate, but was hated by the American boys. This came on the menu with sickening regularity and much of it was heaved overboard."

The 30th had arrived with their standard equipment, but without transportation, machine guns, automatic rifles, Stokes mortars, and 37 mm guns. The British would furnish both motor and animal transportation that would include rolling kitchens and various necessary carts. Vickers and Lewis machine guns would take the place of the U.S. machine guns, automatic rifles, and the 3" Stokers mortars. The American rifles and ammunition would be stored and the troops would use British rifles and ammunition, but the British could not furnish pistols.

The British would also provide all subsistence and the clothing replacement, while the traditional rum ration would be omitted. Ammunition, less pistol, but including 37mm, bombs, grenades, rockets and flares would also be handled by the British. The American infantry would be provided ten weeks of training behind the British lines, with the American commanders retaining full responsibility for the training and discipline, even when affiliated with the British.

From May 22nd through the 28th, the 30th Division would arrive near St. Omer in the British Second Army's area for training. By June 9th, they were still short of their field signal battalion, engineer regiment, one infantry battalion and their sanitary train. On June 14th, the 30th Divisions 105th Engineers would arrive at Calais.

117th soldiers in training on 15 June 1918 with British and Scottish instructors. (U.S. Signal Corps)

Colonel Joseph Hyde Pratt, the commander of the 105th Engineers, would keep a diary of the war which would begin on May 18, 1918, at Camp Sevier. It would detail his entire World War 1 experiences. Several of his entries upon arrival in Europe would include:

"Upon arriving in France we have changed our U.S. rifles for the British rifles. Our men have also given up their barracks bags and all extra clothing has been turned in. The men now carry all their possessions on their backs."

"By June 16 training had begun (sic) with gas school. Mask fitted, tested, and went through the gas house. The mask almost gets the best of me. I nearly suffocate with it and can hardly control myself from tearing it off. This is one of the worst phases of the war for me. Hated to have my men's clothing depleted as was done yesterday. I do not believe they have been left sufficient clothing for their comfort. They now only have two blankets, one suit of clothes and no overcoat. Will not get these again until October 1. The nights are cold and I have slept under three or four blankets."

Elmer Murphy would add in his book that there was considerable grumbling among the men over the British ration.

"Tea and marmalade were unusual and unrelished components of fare in a ration served to American troops upon arrival," he told. "Making the best medical talent available to him General Simmonds studied the British ration thoroughly and then persuaded the British authorities to change several items, among them substituting coffee for tea and to increase the bulk of others so that we finally secured a satisfactory ration that approximated what our troops were accustomed to eating."

On June 21st, and before the completion of their training period, the 30th would move north to the vicinity of Beauval in the British Third Army area. On July 2nd, the 27th Division would move north to the area of the British Second Army, while the 30th would move on toward the British Second Corps area west of Poperinghe, Belgium, to support the British Second Corps in the Ypres sector in an expected German offensive. The 27th National Guard Division had been organized at Camp

Wadsworth, South Carolina, in September, 1917, and would be the only American division that the 30th would have direct contact with for any length of time. The two divisions would be incorporated as the American Second Corps and would be in the same battles throughout the war.

From July 3rd until August 24th, the American troops would train with the British in the forward areas, where on July 9th the American 27th and 30th Divisions would be entrusted with the organization for the East Poperinghe Line, a secondary position in the zone of the British Second Army. On July 4, 1918, the 30th would become the first American force on Belgium soil, where they would be employed in completing an immense trench and wire system to the rear of the 33rd and 49th British Divisions. Following that mission they would receive individual, platoon, and battalion training while on the front line with the 33rd and 49th.

Fighting with British and Australian soldiers (who didn't wear helmets), the 30th would see their first combat on July 9th on defense at the East Poperinghe Line where they would take responsibility for the trench system two days later. Partnered with the British 3rd Division, the 117th Regiment, along with the 59th Brigade, the 30th would reach the front lines in the Canal Sector on July 16, 1918, where they would train and remain until August 18th.

Elmer Murphy would note that on July 23rd one of the pleasant interludes of the training period was the visit of Elsie Janis, the "Sweetheart of the A.E.F.," who came to Watou and there gave her famous entertainment for the men of the 30th Division. Of all the professional entertainers, she alone seemed to be aware that the 30th existed. Then on August 6th, King George, accompanied by a galaxy of ranking British and American officers made a quick inspection of some of the 30th Division and departed as suddenly as he had appeared.

Popular American actress, singer, song writer and screen writer Elsie Janis, "The Sweetheart of the A.E.F" would spend six months entertaining the troops in France. (Elsie Janis' book)

Great Britain's King George would make a quick inspection of Allied Troops on August 6, 1918. (Australian War Memorial)

On the nights of August 16th and 17th, the 30th headed to the front line to relieve the British 33rd at the Canal Sector from around Elenwalle to the railroad southeast of Transport Farm. With the British 6th Division on their right, the 30th would assume command of their sector the next day. On August 19th the Canal Sector would be merged with the Ypres-Lys operations for a distance of 2,400 meters with the 30th, minus its artillery and trains sections. There they would take part in the Ypres-Lys Battle, where as many would drown as were killed. The 119th and 120th Infantry Regiments would aggressively go onto the line, where they would nightly send out strong patrols, primarily to take prisoners who proved difficult to capture. However, the 3rd

Battalion of the 120th did capture one Chinese man whose English vocabulary was apparently limited to "yes" and "Calais."

The 27th and 30th under the British Second Army would continue attacks on August 30th. On the following day, with the 27th (U.S.) on their right and the 14th (G.B.) Division on the left, and with the 59th Brigade in the lead, the 30th would capture all its objectives, including the city of Voormezeele, Lock No. 8 and Lankhof Farm. Their 1,500 yard advance would include the capture of 15 prisoners, 2 machine guns and 35 rifles and a new line was occupied. Beginning on the nights of September 3rd through 5th, the 30th would be relieved by the35th (G.B.) Division, with the 30th being moved to the St. Pol area for training in conjunction with British tanks.

On September 17th the division was moved farther south to join the 27th Division to form the American Second Corps. On September 22 they would join the British Fourth Army in line near Tincourt, northeast of St. Quentin, and prepare to attack the Hindenburg line in the Somme Offensive. There, in conjunction with the Australian corps, their plan of attack was to penetrate the Hindenburg Line and advance on the German railroad center in Maubeuge, France.

On the nights of September 23rd and 24th they would take over a front line sector from the 1st Australian Division. September 25th would see the 27th Division relieve the British 18th and 74th Divisions to the left of the 30th Division, and those British Divisions would pass through the American Second Corps. This movement would allow the American Second Corps to join the Australians where, under the command of Lt. General

Sir John Monash, they would attack against the Hindenburg Line. This would be at the beginning of the Meuse-Argonne Offensive.

Colonel Pratt's diary entry for September 27th would tell:

"Last night about 11:30 p.m. General Lewis phoned over that he wished to see me. When the Commanding General calls for an officer we very often wonder 'what has gone wrong now?' In this case he only wanted to know if I was sure I was going to be able to put out the tape for the 'jumping off line.' I told him not to worry, that I was sure I could do it and do it right. That seemed to relieve him somewhat. Leaving this tape is done in the night before the attack is to commence, and consists of putting a line of white tape (one inch wide) along the whole front of our position just in advance of the front line trench, the object being to give the attacking troops a definite line to form on and to advance uniformly behind the barrage. Outposts will be sent out in advance of this line to prevent the enemy from surprising the taping party. These outposts stay out until just before the attack and then are called in." Colonel Pratt would later report that the tape had been laid out by 4:15 a.m. and that several men, including Lieutenant Griffin, had been gassed.

In a memorandum classified SECRET, Colonel Pratt issued directives for the engineers in support of the attack and the infantry. Company A would be on water supply, while a platoon of Company B was to look for booby traps. Company C was to assist, if necessary in consolidating the line on the right flank, while Company B, less one platoon, was to be held in reserve. A main engineer "dump" would be established as well as two forward regimental dumps. In these dumps, in one-man loads, would be the following: 12,000 shovels, 800 picks, 120 axes, 12,800 sandbags, a possible 6 100-gallon water tanks, 6 windlasses, 4 pumps and 6 horse troughs.

Elmer Murphy's book would state that on August 8th a defense scheme, complete in every detail of the Hindenburg Line between Oise and Bellicourt, had been captured by the British.

The orders for the attack to be launched on September 29th in the direction of Gouy-Nauroy had the American Second Corps (27th and 30th Divisions) on the left and right of the line of the Australian Corps. After the initial objectives were taken, the Australian 3rd and 5th Divisions were to pass through the U.S. divisions to capture the second objective. Beginning on September 26th and 27th, the 30th would assault, beginning about 300 meters east of the line between La Haute Bruyere and Malakoff Farm, with the British 46th on their right and the U.S. 27th to the left. The 59th Brigade and 117th Infantry Regiment would be relieved beginning at night on September 27th. On September 29th, in what would be a major victory, the 30th Division, with the 59th and 60th Infantry Brigades at the front, would push through the Hindenburg line on a curved point in the line in front of the Tunnel of St. Quentin.

This point had been considered impregnable by the Germans because the line curving west of the tunnel consisted of three major trench systems protected by fields heavily covered by barbed wire which had hardly been damaged by artillery fire. Secondly, their higher ground would provide the Germans with devastating fields of machine gun fire, often from concrete emplacements, on any attackers. The enemy trenches also contained a large number of tunnels that led to often electrically-lighted rooms that would hold up to a half-dozen men each. The canal tunnel could shelter a division of men, and also was filled with barges. Numerous other tunnels connected the systems together and included a tunnel to the city of Bellicourt. All through the system were hidden entrances and exits.

The entrance to the Tunnel of St. Quentin on the Hindenburg Line. (Australian War Memorial)

Within the 30th Division, the initial attack was made by the 60th Brigade with the 120th Infantry on the right and the 119th on the left. Each regiment had two battalions in the front line, with one in support. The support battalions were given mopping up missions in the canal tunnel and surrounding Hindenburg Line, as well as in the town of Bellicourt, while the front line battalions would direct certain companies for the mopping up in their area.

The 117th Infantry, along with a company of the division's machine gun battalion, was to follow the 120th Infantry across the tunnel, then turn south following the conclusion of a creeping barrage. During the operation, the mission of the 30th Division would be to protect the flanks of the Australian Division. It was expected that this advance would aid in the crossing of the canal by the British division on the right, where one company of the 120th Infantry, along with a section of machine guns, was to seize and hold the southern exit of the tunnel at Requeval.

For the attack, each soldier would carry 220 rounds of rifle ammunition and two MILLS 23 grenades. Each regiment was to distribute a large load of smoke bombs and red ground flares among its personnel. The smoke bombs would prove useful in clearing out dugouts. For the 96 machine guns, 1,248,000 rounds of ammunition were provided, of which only 156,000 would be left after the attack. Each soldier would also carry one special assault ration as well as an "iron ration," which was a British ration carried in the event of being cut off of regular food supplies. A well-organized supply system would also provide a hot meal to the front line troops on the evening of the battle. This meal would include hard-to-supply fresh meat and would come by horse transportation through rain, mud, and fog over a single road that was also crowded by equipment and troop columns and which underwent constant shelling.

At 5:50 a.m. on September 29th, the 30th Division, supported by 34 British tanks, and including the 60th Brigade and units of the 117th Infantry, assaulted this line on a 3,000 yard front and would capture that entire sector of the Hindenburg system. The heavy fog and smoke would make it extremely difficult for the tanks to follow their directions. One tank commander would report that "it was impossible to see one end of the tank from another." However, it was a common incident for groups of infantry to come across a misplaced tank in the fog and use its assistance in cleaning out a nuisance machine gun nest. The troops would continue their advance to capture the tunnel system.

Men of the American 30th Division and the 8th Tank Corps Battalion of Mark V tanks with "cribs" going forward near Bellicourt on 29 September,1918. (Australian War Memorial)

The 117th Infantry would execute its special mission and would follow the 120th in the morning advance across the Canal Tunnel, where they would turn south and southeast to protect the Division's right flank. Company C, on the right would advance south across the canal bank while Company E on the left would move forward behind the 120th Infantry's right flank toward Nauroy. In their eagerness to push on the tunnels and dugouts in the Hindenburg's defenses, mopping up responsibilities by the 117th were neglected, resulting in the following Australian Divisions being held up by heavy machine gun fire, which the Australians would eventually overcome. By noon the 117th's right flank would connect with the British 46th Division, while its left flank would extend to the 120th Infantry near Nauroy. With their line extended from south of Blacktown and to the western edge of Billiard Copse, the 117th would organize their defensive position.

Finding the enemy position particularly strong around the St. Quentin Canal Tunnel, the Allied attack would push on, leading them to capture the cities of Bellicourt, Nauroy, Requeval, Carriere, Eticourt, Guillaine Ferme and Ferme de Riqueval. This 4,200 yard advance would defeat two enemy divisions and would result in the capture of 1,481 enemy soldiers and much material. One battalion of the 117th Regiment was sent to assist in the mopping up and by 1:30 p.m. the battle at Bellicourt would be considered complete. This victory, and the breaking of the Hindenburg Line, would be prominent in ending the war, and would bring lasting fame to the 30th.

Men of the British 46th Division arriving at the St. Quentin Canal on 2 October 1918 during the attack on the Hindenburg Line. (British Archives)

Captain Nathaniel E. Callen had been with the 117th Regiment since 1906 and would serve along with them during the offensive. He would later be with Infantry School at Fort Benning from 1929-1930, where he would write a monograph for an advanced course that would tell about the battle.

"On September 29, 1918, the battalion (117th and 118th Regiments) as Brigade Reserve had participated in the battle of Bellicourt, more often termed the Breaking of the Hindenburg Line. During this action, its first major offensive, it had had a most valuable experience. Here it had been sent into the fight early with, first the mission of 'mopping up' Bellicourt, and second the mission of attacking unexpected German resistance on the left of our left Brigade. The flank of this brigade was up in the air due to the fact that the attack of the 27th Division had not kept abreast of the 30th. In both these missions it came into hand-to-hand conflict with the Germans so successfully as to make its morale, never very low, hit the ceiling".

Colonel Pratt's diary would tell of his being at Division Headquarter during the battle, where they would receive hourly reports from the battalion commanders.

"Victory was with us right from the start and the division reached all its objectives on time, and went through the Hindenburg Line at its strongest point at Bellicourt. The Germans resisted and we had a good many casualties before the day was over but our men were all game (a little too eager) and determined. 'Remember the Lusitania' and 'Lusitania' were two of the calls the boys gave. When our men had reached their objective, an Australian division went through them and pushed on still further."

Elmer Murphy would record that "prompt and efficient care of the wounded was made a salient part of the plans for battle and the immediate evacuation of those suffering wounds in the battle of Bellicourt is characteristic of the efficiency of the Medical

Corps of the 30th Division. With the advance of the troops, aid stations and ambulance posts were rushed forward. At approximately an hour after the battle began the first casualties were at advanced dressing stations and within one and one-half hours, walking casualties began to arrive at the walking wounded station. By nightfall all of the 2,575 wounded during the day's fighting had been given medical attention and afforded all possible surcease from their pains. At the advanced main dressing stations, patients and troops were served during the day over 5,000 hot meals."

A wounded American soldier being assisted by an Australian soldier at the Battle of Bellicourt. (Australian War Memorial)

Following the breakthrough, the Australian 5th Division would pass through the 30th and beginning on October 1st and 2nd the 30th would be relieved and moved back to Herbecourt. Captain Callen would comment about the 30th's deserved break.

"In execution of the 'rest plan' billeting parties were hurriedly assembled on October 1st and sent to the new areas. On October 2nd our regiment followed by marching. This march was completed, after marching all day under heavy pack at about 1030 p.m. on the night of October 2nd and we still found ourselves on the old Somme Battlefield. We had marched almost 30 kilometers under pack and were thoroughly tired out, so without bothering to locate even the limited shelter our billeting party had found, we curled up and slept. Such a night's rest, out of hearing of battle, worked wonders and early the next morning all were up for a hot meal and to locate new quarters, avail ourselves of a bath in a nearby stream, get into clean clothes, shave and write letters home."

"We found that the area we had been given was indeed possessed of little accommodations in the way of shelter and during the day we had to resort to the pup tents for a camp. We could, however have access to our kitchens and to plenty of clear, cold water for washing and baths. Everyone pitched in and by night a surprising amount of cheerfulness was noticeable throughout the command."

On October 3rd the 30th Division commander issued orders for the division to prepare to relieve the Australian 2nd Division on the front line near Montbrehain beginning on October 5th. This time individual regiments of the Division would move by bus or trucks on the nights of October 5th through the 8th.

Having been informed on October 4th that the Division was being moved by truck beginning the next morning, he believed that the destination would be an area better suited for the needs of the troops. On October 5th he would state that in the morning "all necessary embossing orders having been (sic) published the preceding night, we found our busses (motor trucks and or London Double Decker Buses) assembled at 8 a.m. on the road through our area and the battalion having previously been formed in groups of four squads to the truck were loaded and on the move into the general column by 8:20 a.m."

The Lewis guns with which each company was equipped were permitted to be loaded on the transports, while troops turned out in full equipment and with 160 rounds of ammunition per man. In addition, each squad had two cooked meals along with their "iron" ration. The combined column would pull out promptly at 8:30 a.m. and would soon catch up with the other units. Moving in a northeasterly direction, they would again pass through Perrone where they would take a more eastward road. Since the Somme Valley had been fought over throughout the war, there was no vegetation and one could see for miles over the gently rolling hills.

At around 4 p.m. the troops would become more alert when they passed through ruins that had once been the town of Roisel, which they had earlier passed through on their way to Bellicourt. They then began to realize that their well-earned rest might not be the purpose of the move. The convoy would continue on until it reached Rossou, just four kilometers from Bellicourt, where the men were ordered off the buses and into columns to march on the road leading to Bellicourt.

The men began the march under British regulations, with four men abreast and dressed to the right, and with the leading guide marching as far to the right as possible. Platoons were kept 50 yards apart, with the Company and Platoon Commanders in the rear of their commands. The columns would halt for a ten minute rest each hour, where they would clear the road. It was forbidden to make up for lost distance during the breaks and when marching, the men were expected to stay in step with their platoons and carry their arms in a uniform manner. Arriving in Bellicourt, the column ran into a traffic jam heading to the rear, as well as transports moving forward, and a long halt was required.

After the halt had continued for some time, Captain Callen moved to the head of the column in the hopes of getting some information as to the destination from the Regiment. Upon arriving at the front, he would find that the Commanding Officer was with the brigade commander and had left instructions with his Lieutenant Colonel that he was to lead the regiment clear of the town and clear of the road and await orders. Captain Callen continued his story:

"While in column off the right of the road and before the traffic jam had been cleared, we had our first and only experience of being machine gunned and bombed from the air while we were on the march".

"Two German planes flying in tandem struck the head of the leading battalion and traversed the column from head to rear, raking it first or in front of the nose of the plane with machine guns leaving a rain of bombs in their rear. The leading battalions together with the jammed transportation being on the streets of Bellicourt and unable to spread out suffered severely. Our own battalion fortunately was not so cooped up, being still clear of the town and only had one man hit.

"Needless to say the planes were not molested and in addition to getting a relatively large number of casualties, both in men and animals, they also succeeded in completely blocking progress for some time on this particular road.

"We had not been trained at that time in organized anti-aircraft combat so the planes were unmolested. In addition to all this, they of course were informed that a considerable number of troops were headed toward the front and they later shelled the forward areas vigorously until daylight."

Captain Callen would recall that the men had finished their evening meal, filled their canteens and had fallen asleep when they were soon awakened. The tired men got to their feet and onto the road with little delay and marched through Nauroy toward Estrees, where American and Australian guides awaited them on the outskirts of Estrees. Due to the extreme dangers of shelling the troops left the road and split into companies, where they were guided more or less across country to their positions on the line. The companies were later broken up into much smaller units due to the heavy German artillery fire which began to fall over the entire rear area of the unit.

That shelling, which spread three kilometers from the line to the rear areas, began around 12:00 midnight and even after companies had split into smaller sections, they still suffered casualties. In M Company a single shell would take out 16 men and a lieutenant.   Some companies were finally reaching their destinations at 4:00 a.m., where, as tired as they were, they all dug some type of foxhole or were lucky enough to take cover with the Australian soldiers. On the line the Americans had double the number of troops that the Australians had, with the American battalions having 28 officers and a little more than 1,000 men that included medical and signal detachments.

Leaving a minimum number of guards, the tired men went to sleep instead of waiting for a breakfast they did not have. Some men who didn't know the direction to the enemy and were not sufficiently covered became sniper casualties in the early morning. With the ground being nearly empty of hedges or fences, a man who could be seen would become a casualty.

The Germans on the front held a strong and deep position along the bank of a railroad and another to the rear along the bank of an improved road, all southwest of the Mons Road. To the northeast of the road the Germans occupied a sugar factory and several nearby buildings to the rear of the factory. They also had a small force behind the fill on the improved road that led across the Allied sector at Montbrehain. Another large force was dug in just behind the sugar factory on the railroad.

The morning of October 6th would clear enough to make the Allied positions very visible. Some men had dug under cover but those of the extra platoon did not provide the necessary cover for the enemy on the left flank. The morning would begin with men wanting to eat, needing water or wondering what to do with their wounded. The men had eaten their last cooked meal the evening before, then marched five and a half kilometers, had been on the move since the morning and had taken nearly a hundred casualties, all on one canteen of water per man.

The deadly fire from the enemy made it obvious that no food or water could be brought to them, and many of the wounded could not be reached to be tended to. Medical assistance was promised for those most critical, but some would die before being reached by a battalion surgeon. On October 6th at 11:00 p.m. orders were given to attack at 5:10 the next morning.

For the 30th Division, the 117th Infantry Regiment would have one battalion on the front line, with one in support and one in reserve. On the right, the 118th Infantry would have two battalions on the front line with one battalion in support. During the morning attack the American Second Corps would advance the line slightly northwest of Montbrehain where they would fight back a counterattack. For its part, the 30th Division would advance 500 yards on a 1,200 yard front northwest of Montbrehain, where they would capture 150 prisoners. The enemy would counterattack, but would be beaten back. The captured prisoners reported that they had been expecting an attack since the morning of October 6th, and had been slowly withdrawing their forces.

The report to headquarters that day told that the 59th Brigade had advanced under an artillery barrage, while the 60th Brigade remained in the Hargicourt-Bellicourt areas with the exception of the 1st Battalion of the 120th Infantry which had marched to a point southeast of Nauroy to serve as a reserve for the 59th Brigade. Reported as able for duty were 514 officers and 16,356 men of the 30th Division.

Captain Callen would provide some interesting light on the attack after he and his four company commanders headed to a conference with his Colonel and a British Artillery Liaison Officer. Callen would state,

"We were informed that we were to attack at 5:10 a.m. on the following morning in order to bring our position up with the 118th Infantry on our right and with the British on our left. Here the Colonel was rudely interrupted by several of us at once desiring to know who told him the British had advanced on our left. He replied that they, the British, had attacked on the previous afternoon before our arrival and had captured the town of Breaurevoir and advanced their lines to the towns of Poncheux and Geneve. We in turn insisted that this was absolutely false, but that if they had, that they had been firing on us all during the day with disastrous results. This verified by the commanding officers of Companies I and L. This left the colonel quite excited and the call for the British Intelligence Summary for the period. Summary very clearly stated that the British continuing their attack on the afternoon of the 5th of October had captured the town of Beaurevoir and had advanced their lines abreast of town of Poncheux. The colonel was at a loss to decide what to do and we advised against any such attack.

"On the other hand our orders coming from division through brigade were explicit and our mission to attack at 5:10 a.m. 7th October advance our lines to the line Ponchaux-Geneve-Montbrehain were clear cut and definite. Time was midnight or thereabout. We knew the location of brigade headquarter, but not division, and being connected to brigade by the telephone the colonel consented to call the brigade commander and inform him of the situation.

"For this purpose he left us for a few minutes and returned and informed us he was very sorry, but that it was too late to make any change of plans and that the attack must be made.

"We were dumfounded and with all vehemence we could, insisted that it could not be done. To attempt to execute this would force the battalion to expose its entire lines in prolongation to strong positions held by German machine guns and riflemen during the entire advance, in addition to the fire coming from the Germans within our sector. We further pointed out that the objective, as designated, did not even permit our advance to all prepared enemy positions on our front but contemplated our digging into an unprepared position just a matter of a few hundred yards from where they lay unmolested, in positioning fire upon the men so engaged. The colonel still felt it would be a reflection on the regiment if we did not make the attack and still insisted that it must be done. I frankly say, without meaning to criticize any higher authority, that none of the higher commanders, who by reason of their rank and duties, has never felt the weight of fire from a well-disposed enemy, could visualize how serious this situation was. In a dim way this realization came to us that night as we tried from our subordinate positions to secure relief from such foolish and impossible tasks."

Feeling defeated in their task, the officers then asked for tanks, which were denied, and for machine gun support, which was also denied with the reasoning that they would be needed during the general attack on October 8th. Some assurance came when the British Artillery Officer cheerfully assured the men that they would provide a rolling artillery barrage with all the fire that they needed. The officers then asked the British officer if the fire could include the area on their left to include the cemetery east of Beaurevoir and the known enemy position along the railroad in the village of Poncheux, all of which was in their sector of responsibility. This request was denied because of a report that the areas were already held by British troops.

Just as the officers were leaving, the Colonel called Captain Callan aside to tell him that if the situation demanded it, he would send up to two companies from the 2nd Battalion reserve, if they were requested. Seeing that this offer was of no use, Callen pressed the Colonel to send up the trench mortar squad from Headquarters Company and this request was agreed upon.

By this time the supply service had managed to provide the front line troops with food and some water. With Zero Hour soon approaching, the captain and his lieutenants could do little more than return to their troops and wait for the 5:10 a.m. attack. Prior to the attack, Captain Callen would make a reconnaissance of the dugouts and shelters of Advance Division Battle P.C. at Nauroy, and would tell that the troops were moving forward so quickly that it was difficult to keep supplies to the front. Colonel Pratt would later state that he had spent a large part of the day in the forward area between Bellicourt and Nauroy.

The battle plan for October 7th was for Brancourt le Grand to be reached by the assault troops following behind a barrage. The 59th Infantry Brigade was to lead the attack with the 1st Battalion of the 117th Infantry in the lead, with the 2nd Battalion in support, and the 118th Infantry with the 2nd and 3rd Battalions in the lead and the 1st Battalion in support. The Brigade Reserve would consist of the 117th's 3rd Battalion and the 120th's 1st Battalion.

The Brigade's machine gun companies were to support the attack, with two companies of the 114th Machine Gun Battalion given the special mission of securing the Division's flanks. One battalion of tanks was assigned to accompany the assault troops, while two companies of light tanks were to assist in the exploitation of the attack objectives.

Led by the 59th on October 8th, the 30th would attack each day through the 11th to take the towns of Premont and Brancourt in an advance of 17,500 yards that would see the capture of a number of other areas and small towns and the taking of 1,944 prisoners. During the operation they would encounter units of 14 different German divisions.

The attack would begin at the 5:10 a.m. given time in conjunction with the British 6th and 25th Divisions on the right and left. At the beginning of the attack, the 30th Division's 118th Infantry, which was on the right, would soon meet strong resistance on the western outskirts of Brancourt le Grand. Their advance would be held up until they were joined by a company of the 118th Infantry's 1st Battalion and elements from the 120th Infantry's 1st Battalion. This would allow the town to be mopped up and occupied, with the normal objective being met by 11:00 a.m.

To the left, the 117th Infantry's 1st Battalion would reach their objective about 7:30 a.m., where it would be passed through by the 2nd Battalion at around 8:10 a.m. The 2nd Battalion would continue and would control and occupy Premont by 11:30 a.m.

By 12:30 p.m. the line was reported to be consolidated and an advance was made east of Premont that met no resistance.

The 30th Division would continue to attack daily until relieved by the 27th Division during the night of October 11th and 12th, and command would be passed to the 27th on that morning. The 30th would then assemble in the area of Bonhain-Premonte-Busigny, where it would serve as the corps reserve until returning to the same position on October 16th.

The British 4th Army would issue orders for an attack to be a part of the general offensive on the British 4th and French 1st Army's front, with the task of the II Corp to attack abreast with the 30th on the right. The 30th was then assigned to take over a portion of the zone held by the 27th on the night of October 15th and 16th. The 30th Division's 59th Infantry Brigade was directed to attack behind a barrage and tanks to capture the towns of Molain and St. Martin Riviere, and move on to their first objective, which was a northwest running line that passed through the outskirts of Ribbeuville. After a halt of three hours, the 60th Infantry would pass through the 59th toward the second objective, which was a north-south line running through La Haie Tonnoile Ferme. After finishing this second objective, patrols were to be sent to the line of the Sambre Canal, which was just east of Catillon.

The preliminary bombardment of the attack would begin at 8 a.m. on October 16th, with the time for the attack set for 5:20 a.m. the next morning. The American II Corps would be reinforced by the Australian 3rd and 5th Division's artillery, along with that of the 2nd and 4th Australian Divisions, which were already attached.

The attack formation would include the 59th Infantry Brigade's 117th Infantry with the 2nd Battalion in the lead and supported by the 3rd Battalion, and the 118th Infantry's 3rd Battalion plus Company E of the 1st Battalion, with the 2nd Battalion, less Company E, in support.

The attack would begin on time but enemy fire and early fog would cause difficulty in crossing the Selle River. While this would cause some units to lose their direction, the delay would also cause the leading units to lose the effects of the barrage. Heavy machine gun fire on their front and right flank would temporarily stall the 117th Infantry which were to the right of the attack. The 1st Battalion would soon be strengthened by the 2nd and 3rd Battalions and the three would become a part of the line by 10:00 a.m. By 11:30 a.m. the three battalions had crossed the Selle and moved forward to the line of the railroad, where fire from Ribeauville would stop any further advance, leaving the regiment to entrench around 12:30 p.m. Units on the right and left would come forward to the 117th's line around 4:00p.m. and close the gap on its flanks.

At 5 p.m. the 60th Infantry Brigade was directed by the division to relieve the 59th Brigade at dusk and this was completed around 4 a.m. on October 18th. The 59th would then be withdrawn to the Division's reserve. The 119th Infantry would relieve the 117th on the right half zone and the 120th Infantry would relieve the 118th in the left half. While the relief was occurring the 60th Infantry was ordered by the division to continue the attack at 5:30 a.m., with the day's objective being a north/south line about one kilometer east of Mazinghien. Exploitation to the canal was to be attempted, with the attack to be preceded by a rolling barrage.

The 120th Infantry would also attack at 5:30 a.m. and would advance beyond the Ribeville-l' Arbe de Guise road and would meet little opposition, while the 119th had not yet advanced. By 10:00 a.m. the visibility had improved to where the 120th would be hit by heavy shelling, which forced it to withdraw to the original line of departure. The 120th would advance again at 6:00 p.m. and would reach a line that extended northwest to the vicinity of Ecaillon Hameau by 8:30 p.m., where it would remain for the night.

By 1:30 a.m. on October 19 the 119th Infantry would pass through Ecallion, where it would receive the order to halt and consolidate. That morning at 5:30 the 60th Brigade would continue the attack, with the high ground overlooking the Sambre Canal being their objective. By 10:00 a.m. Mazinghien had been passed and the assault would encounter heavy fire at 2:30 p.m. that would hold both regiments up. As preparations were being made to overcome the opposition, orders would be received to hold the ground until they could be relieved by British 1st Division. That relief would be completed over the night of October 19-20th over a line that roughly extended from Rejet-de-Beaulieu-Mazinghien for nearly a kilometer southeast of la Jon Quiere Farm. In those three days of attacks against three German divisions, the 30th would advance a further 9,000 yards. Much of the fighting from October 8th through the 19th would occur over uneven terrain and through small patches of woods and villages and an occasional small town.

Often without artillery support, they would be going against heavy machine gun defenses and would have to cross the banks of the heavily defended Selle River. During this 20 mile advance the 30th would suffer over 8,000 casualties, but would capture nearly 4,000 of the enemy, along with much equipment. The success of the 30th could only be explained by the American toughness, skill with their weapons, and dogged determination.

American soldiers being prepared for burial after the Battle of the Hindenburg Line. (Australian War Memorial)

During that last operation the advance had been so rapid and the troops withdrawn so quickly that there was no opportunity to gather up captured artillery, mortars, machine guns, rifles and other materials. In fact, on some occasions the captured artillery would be used by the Allies to fire on the retreating Germans.

Now relieved, the 30th would assemble in the vicinity of St. Souplet, before moving to the Tincour-Brouely area, where it would remain through October 22nd. On October 23rd the 30th Division would then be withdrawn to the HeillyTraining Area near Amiens for a well-earned rest and replacements. Two weeks later and just as an order to return to the front was expected, the Armistice would be signed on November 11th, the war would end and the 30th had ended its last combat service of the war. During the war and after having endured bombings, shelling, gassings, trench attacks and hand-to-hand combat, the 30th would suffer heavy casualties, with 1,237 killed in action and 7,178 wounded in action.

Worthy of mention were the "other" casualties that were listed under "troops not in divisions." Many of these were men who had gone Absence Without Leave (AWOL) from their rear echelon divisions to desert to the front. Finding their way to the front, many would take part in the fighting, with some killed or wounded. These cases would become so numerous that General Pershing would make special arrangements by which trained men with good service could be rewarded with the opportunity to take part in the fighting at the front.

Of the 2,084,000 American soldiers who reached France, 1,390,000 would see active service on the front line. During the war, twelve members of the 30th would receive the Medal of Honor (four of which were posthumous). Throughout the war, the 30th Division would become the only wholly American division to be honored by a review from King George.

References:

Callen,Nathaniel E. "Monograph of the Operations of the 3rd Battalion 117th Infantry 30th Division".

Lillard, Stewart. "Highway 30: The David Wiley Memorial Highway", Tennessee Ancestors, December 2010.

Moore, William E. and Russell, James C., "U.S. Official Pictures of the World War", Pictorial Bureau, Washington D.C., 1920

Murphy, Elmer A. and Thomas, Robert S. "The Thirtieth Division in the World War", Old Hickory Publishing Company, Arkansas, 1936.

Pratt, Colonel Joseph Hyde, Commander of the 105th Engineers. "His Diary".

30th Division, "Summary of Operations in the World War", prepared by the American Battle Monuments Commission created by Congress in 1923.

Chapter Four

SERGEANT EDWARD ROBERT TALLEY

World War I Medal of Honor recipient, Sergeant Edward R. Talley (Bill Moore)

Edward Robert Talley was born at Russellville, Tennessee on September 8, 1890, one of the eight children of farmer John Elijah Talley and his wife, Ellen Seaver Talley. The family would include sons Elmer, Erbin, Earl, Edward, Frank, Charles and John Henry and daughter Lilly (Horner). As was common at the time, young children were quickly put to work on the farm while attending small neighborhood schools. A side benefit to the farm work would be that the hard labor would develop hardy adults.

  After attending the old Russellville High School, Edward would take a mining job in Virginia. He returned to Tennessee for road construction work with R.L. Peters and Tracy Prater, and later had a job as a brakeman on the C & O Railroad. During that time he would join the National Guard, which then was a good social outlet, as well as a chance to make a little extra money. On February 2, 1918, as America's involvement in World War I was growing, the 27 year-old Edward would marry schoolteacher Mattie Moore who was from nearby Whitesburg.

Whitesburg school teacher Mattie Moore who would become the wife of Edward R. Talley. (Bill Moore)

Inducted into the Army on May 11, 1917, Talley would report for duty with the 82nd Division, 327th Infantry, Machinegun Company at Camp Gordon, Georgia where his age and prior military experience would soon see him being promoted to Sergeant. While at Camp Gordon, Talley would begin his training. Following a vaccination, he would write Mattie a post card telling her that "I am so sick I can hardly stand up."

At the time the 30th Infantry Division which had originally been a National Guard division with units in Tennessee and North and South Carolina was being formed at Camp Sevier, South Carolina. In October, 1917, draftees, from the Midwest, along with the 82nd from Georgia, would be sent to fill out the vacancies in the 30th Infantry Division. The division would officially get the nickname, "The Old Hickory Division" on 26 March, 1918.

Newly married Edward R. Talley and Mattie Moore Talley on her visit to Talley's Army Camp in 1918. (Bill Moore)

Arriving at Camp Sevier, Talley would be assigned to the 30th Division's 3rd Battalion, 117th Regiment, Company L. There, beginning on the first part of May 1918, the 30th would board trains for Hoboken and New York City to sail for England. Soon after their arrival in England and a brief stay in rest camps, they proceeded on to Folkstone to cross the Channel to Calais, France.

From Calais, they would move near St. Omer to be billeted with the British Second Army at the Eperlecques Training Area, where their American equipment would be stored and exchanged for British weapons. There, British instructors would begin training them in the trench warfare system. On June 21st, before their training was completed, the 30th would move north to the vicinity of Beauval to the British 3rd Army area. On July 2nd they would move toward the British Second Corps in the Ypres sector, where they would join the American 27th Division to form the U.S. Second Corps, and would fight together throughout the war.

From July 3rd until August 24th, the Second Corps would join with the British in the forward areas, where on July 9th the Second Corps would be charged with organizing the East Poperinghe Line, a secondary line of the British 2nd Army. Fighting with British and Australian soldiers, they would see combat in the defense of the East Poperinghe Line. By July 16th, they would reach the front lines of the Canal Sector, where they would train and remain until August 18th.

After weeks of behind the line training by the British Second Corps in the Poperinghe area, elements of the 30th Division would see action in a gas attack against the Germans on August

26th and 27th in the Ypres-Lys Offensive. They would again see action at Ypres on August 1st through the 4th and Dickebusch Lake on August 7th through 9th.

That action would be followed by further training in rear areas not subject to shell fire. On September 22nd the 30th Division would move into the Canal area to be positioned alongside the U.S. 27th Division and the British 46th Division for the assault on the Hindenburg Line. The Battle of Bellicourt would be fought on September 29th and 30th, and on October 2nd the 30th would move back for a rest. It was soon recalled to the lines on October 5th and 6th. On the 7th the Division was again fighting, when at 5:15 A.M. Company L of the 117th Infantry was ordered to go "over the top."

It was on October 7th near Poncheaux, about 100 miles north of Paris, where Sergeant Talley had been watching his comrades being ripped by enemy machinegun fire. Grabbing his bolt-action rifle, he charged into the fire, killing or wounding six of the enemy. His continued fire kept a second machinegun crew from setting up and his efforts would save a number of his fellow soldiers. This action would earn Talley the Medal of Honor, while the 30th had been a part of breaking the Hindenburg Line at the St. Quentin Canal.

Later, on January 6, 1919, Colonel Gary F. Spence, commander of the 117th Infantry Regiment, would give a delayed account of the battle. He would tell of Talley's Company L Commander, Captain David Lillard, being wounded on October 7th, on the day that Talley would earn his medal. Lillard would eventually recover and live until 1954.

"On the morning of October 7, 1918, when Capt. David W. Lillard was directed to attach to and straighten out a line near Poncheaux, France, his company was moving forward under heavy machine gun and trench mortar fire and reached within 75 yards of its objective (a railroad cut), when Capt. Lillard was hit by a machine gun bullet which exploded two magazine clips containing fourteen shells. All of these shells entered his body, making a fearful wound. Although terribly wounded and knocked down, he got to his knees and waved and directed the further advance of his company to its objective. He then, while lying on the ground, wrote three orders and sent runners for assistance. The fire was so intense that his orderly carried him about 75 yards to the rear of a shell hole where he was unconscious for a few minutes. Regaining consciousness he continued in command of his company, issuing verbal orders from time to time and remaining in command for about six hours."

Captain David Lillard, Commander of Talley's Company L, would be seriously wounded on October 7. His recovery would be lengthy. (Tennessee Ancestors)

The linear calendar reference for October 8, 1918, kept by the 30th Division, would briefly describe the battle as follows:

"Our troops advanced yesterday morning in the face of strong machine gun fire and straightened out our front east and north of Mont Brehaim (sic). All objectives taken with the exception of a small part on our left. 277 prisoners were taken; our casualties 8 officers 213 men. The advance was about 500 yards on a front of 1,200 yards. Hostile counterattacks repulsed."

In a summation report, Col. Spence (117th Infantry) and Major General Edward Lewis (30th Division commander) attempted to establish correct figures for the 117th Infantry and the 59th Brigade. In the Beaurevoir sector, the units would advance 17,500 yards on October 8-9th, at the expense of 18 officers and 403 enlisted men killed, 28 officers and 587 enlisted men severely wounded, ten officers and 857 enlisted men slightly wounded, five officers and 370 enlisted men gassed, 100 enlisted men missing and five enlisted men taken prisoner by the Germans.

Fighting would continue at Busigny on October 16th and 17th, Molain on October 18th and Ribeauville on October 19th and 20th. By then Talley's company was exhausted but the Hindenburg Line had been broken. On October 20th, his exhausted company, which had taken heavy casualties, would come off the front line for a rest, where they would be while the Armistice was being signed on November 11, 1918.

Major General Lewis would later conclude that the entire 30th Division had a total of 8,415 casualties during the war and that the division had smashed through one of the strongest defense systems in the entire Hindenburg Line.

Following the Armistice, Sergeant Talley, along with other American forces would be involved in repair and restoration work before boarding a ship at St. Nazaire on March 18, 1919, for the voyage back to America, where they would land at Charleston, South Carolina. Sent on from Camp Jackson, South Carolina he would be mustered out of the service at Fort Oglethorpe, Georgia, on April 25, 1919.

Back at home, Sergeant Talley would choose to receive his Medal of Honor which was presented by Lt. Colonel Andrew J. White at Russellville High School. The event would become an all-day festival with people coming from miles around to witness the ceremony.

Following the reading of Talley's Medal of Honor citation, Lieutenant Colonel White would place the medal, hung from blue ribbon, around Talley's neck. That medal would stay In the Talley home, along with a large portrait of the hero, for many years before being displayed at Morristown's Rose Center Museum. That medal and portrait are no longer displayed.

The Medal of Honor that was presented to Sergeant Edward R. Talley.

In addition to the Medal of Honor, Talley would receive a number of foreign decorations that would include the French Croix de Guerre with Palm, the Belgian Croix de Guerre with Silver Star, the Portuguese War Cross of the Third Class, the British Military Medal, the Italian Cross of Military Valor, the French Medaille Militaire and the Montenegrin Medaille Pour La Bravoure Militaire.

Mattie Moore Talley and Edward R. Talley shortly after he had received the Medal of Honor in 1919. (Bill Moore)

Edward would make good use of his mustering out pay of $3,037.87, a significant sum in that day. Shortly after receiving his medal, Edward and Mattie, along with his brother Frank, would move to Appalachia, Virginia, where both brothers opened stores and where Edward became a successful merchant at his store on Callahan Avenue. After building 11 rental houses alongside his store and on the riverbank, the area would be called "Talley Town" for many years.

While living in Appalachia, Edward and Mattie would attend a number of military commemorations including one early October trip to Cleveland, Ohio. In Cleveland Edward would participate in a parade of 20,000 Legionnaires and would be among the 31 Medal of Honor recipients in the parade. At the end of the celebration, Edward and Mattie would take a steamer to Buffalo, New York, to spend a day at Niagara Falls.

Throughout their time in Appalachia, the Talleys would often return to Russellville in their van for a load of meat and produce to sell in their store. With the coming of Cherokee Lake in 1942, they would frequently return for camping trips with relatives, where Edward would fry the fish he had caught for breakfast.

Renting his store to a nephew, Edward and Mattie would return to Russellville for good in 1945, where he would open a store and build a home on their 66 acre farm. (That still-standing home has currently been modified into the Allen's Funeral Home building. Edward would also take over the operation of the former C & S Market, which sat across Highway 11-E from their home. He would soon turn over much of the operation of his store in order to spend more time on his farm, with Wylie Seals being the last manager of the store while it was under Talley's ownership.

While Edward and Mattie had no children of their own, they would enjoy spending time with their nieces and nephews. Niece Mary Alice Harville, (nee) Moore, Moore would stay with them during her school years at Morristown. Other nieces and nephews would often stay for the weekends, where they were often treated with candy from the store and half-dollars from "Uncle Ed."

The front of Ed and Mattie Moore Talley's Russellville home. (Bill Moore)

Edward R. Talley tends to his pigs on his Russellville, Tennessee farm. (Mary Alice Harville)

Edward would tell that he and Calvin Ward, Hamblen County's other Medal of Honor recipient, had known each other slightly before the war. In his later years, he and Ward would sometimes sit together at Morristown's Roddy's Pool Room to talk and watch the pool games.

On November 27, 1950, Edward Talley, who had been suffering from a liver ailment, would enter the Mountain Home Veterans Hospital at Johnson City, where he would pass away on December 14, 1950, at age 60. Mattie had been staying with him during his illness. At his request, he would be buried with military honors provided by the American Legion Post 52, at Whitesburg's historic Bent Creek Cemetery, where he would be joining soldiers dating back to the Revolutionary War.

Edward R. Talley enjoying some time on his tractor at his Russellville, Tennessee farm. (Mary Alice Harville)

In 1953, then-governor Frank Clement would send a National Guard plane for Talley's wife, Mattie, and his niece, Mary Alice, to be put up at the Waldorf Astoria Hotel in New York as Walter Winchell's personal guests at the "Bravest and Finest" program that saluted America's foremost heroes. Edward R. Talley would be honored by a bridge in his name at Kyle's Ford in Hancock County, Tennessee, as well as a recreation Center in Morristown, which would carry his and Calvin Ward's name. In the years that would follow, both men would largely be forgotten until 2015 when two bridges on Highway 25 in Morristown, would each carry their individual names.

Although Talley did receive some accolades and attention in the years immediately following the war, he never received the wide spread fame one would expect for such valor. He spent most of his post-war life in obscurity, mostly by his own choosing.

Medal of Honor recipient Sergeant Edward R. Talley's grave at Whitesburg's Bent Creek Cemetery. (Claborn)

References:

Hill, Howard. "E.R. Talley, Winner of Medal of Honor", Morristown Daily Gazette Mail, November 22, 1959.

Jacobs, Bruce. Letter to Mr. Edward Talley. Undated.

Lillard, Stewart. "Highway 30: The David Wiley Memorial Highway", Tennessee Ancestors, December 2010.

Moore, William E. and Russell, James C. "U.S. Official Pictures of the World War", Pictorial Bureau, Washington, D.C., 1920.

National Personnel Record Center, St. Louis, Missouri.

*30th Division, "Summary of Operations in the World War",
prepared by the American Battle Monuments Commission,
created by Congress in 1923.*

Chapter Five

PRIVATE CALVIN JOHN WARD

Medal of Honor recipient Private Calvin Ward would be born in Greene County and would list Morristown, Tennessee as his home. (National Archives.)

The only son of Alvin Lewis and Laura Magnolia Ward's eight children, Calvin Ward was born on October 30, 1899, in his grandfather Ephriam's log cabin on a small Guthrie's Gap hilltop on the edge of Tennessee's Greene County near Bull's Gap. With his birth recorded in the family Bibles as "John Calvin,"

Ward would sometimes list his name as "Calvin John." His sisters were Essie, Maxine, Mabel, Cleo, Georgia, Mary and Nola. Mother Laura, born at Bulls Gap in 1873, would die at Bristol, Virginia on February 19, 1951, while her husband, Alvin, born April 3, 1870, would pass away at Bristol on July 3, 1949. Both would be buried at Bristol's Glenwood Cemetery.

The June 4, 1900 census would find seven months-old Calvin living with his family at "Whitesburg Village" near Bull's Gap. With the closeness to Bulls Gap, the Ward family would naturally use the town for selling their produce and buying their necessities. By the April, 1910 census, the 10 year old Calvin was living with his family in Greene County, most likely in the Mount Hope community near Mohawk. That same census told that Calvin had attended school but could not write. Soon afterwards, the family would move to Hamblen County's Valley Home Road and on to a two-story house on the corner of Morristown's 748 First North Street. At age 14 he would be stricken with typhoid fever, but would recover.

In Morristown, a young Calvin would work for the Dougherty Brothers Table Shop on Mill Street, which was followed by a job with the Southern Railway. Seventeen year-old Calvin was living near a sister in Cincinnati, Ohio, when he would enlist in the Army on July 7, 1917, in the Truck Company of No. 5 Division Supply Train, 16th Division. He would list Morristown, Tennessee as his home town. By July 29th, he would be dropped from the company as a deserter.

Calvin Ward's parents, Lewis and Laura Ward. (Cleo Sipe Purkey)

In that time he had returned to Morristown where he is shown to have become a member of Company D, 117th Infantry Regiment of the Tennessee National Guard on July 14th, which would be federalized on July 25, 1917. Upon his entrance physical doctors would find that he had a rare condition, Dexter Cardia, which meant that his heart was on the right side of his body. Soon sent to Camp Sevier, South Carolina, the 117th would be a part of the 30th Infantry Division. The new soldiers began the difficult task of being disciplined by "home folks," of which a few had been semi-trained by recent service with General Pershing on the Mexican border. With the great demand for uniforms, many of the new soldiers learned military drill in their civilian clothes.

In March, 1918, Calvin was being charged for being absent without leave. Orders for the 117th to be shipped to Europe allowed Calvin to escape a three month sentence in the Camp Sevier guard house when he boarded the ship with the rest of the regiment. The men had boarded the Northumberland, formerly a cattle boat that had been captured in the war and converted to a troop ship, for the Atlantic crossing.

Arriving in Britain, Calvin's division was soon moved to Calais, France, where bombing raids showed them the deficiencies in their prior training. By September 29th, they were deeply involved in the stark and bitter conflict at the Battle of Bellicourt during the Meuse-Argonne Offensive. There they would rupture the strong German line in a fierce battle full of individual hells. Ward's Company D would be pulled back from the front on October 1st, but 4 days later they would be back at the front for a seven day conflict that would be an assault on the strongest part of the enemy's Hindenburg Line and which would later be known as the Battle of Montbrehain. It was there on October 8th that Calvin would earn the Medal of Honor.

That event would occur near Estreess, France on the morning of October 8, 1918, when the small remainder of Calvin's detachment was pinned down in a muddy shell hole by machine guns on either side. "We'd had enough," Sgt. James Ernest "Buck" Karnes would say. Along with Sgt. Karnes, and armed with his rifle and a bag of grenades, Ward would crawl along shell holes until he could demolish a German position with a grenade. Both men would then leap into the position to kill three of the enemy and take seven prisoners before silencing a second machine gun. The efforts of Ward and Karnes would free their company to advance against the German lines in the war's last major offensive.

Knoxville's Sergeant James E. Buck Karnes would be with Calvin Ward when both men would earn the Medal of Honor. (National Archives)

The day had also been costly for the Americans, with the company's strength being reduced from 200 to 34 men. Five days later Ward would be gassed but, after being treated in the field, he would rejoin the fighting which would finally end with the signing of the Armistice on November 11, 1918. Morristown boys of Ward's Company D, Bruce M. Colboch and Gray Harris, would be killed in action on October 8th while Tip M. Allen would die from his wounds the next day.

World War I doughboys who had been fighting "Over There" were eager to leave France to go home. They were in formation on February 9, 1919, while General John. J. 'Black Jack' Pershing was awarding decorations. In that formation Pershing would present Morristown, Tennessee's Private Calvin Ward with his Medal of Honor.

Another Tennessean, Sgt. Alvin C. York, had been awarded the Distinguished Service Cross on November 30th, 1918. Papers were submitted to have that award rescinded and changed to the Medal of Honor. After a thorough investigation, the paper work was finally submitted to President Wilson on March 20th, 1919. The award of the Medal of Honor was approved and was presented to York on April 18th, 1919. On hand at the time was a Saturday Evening Post writer, George Patullo, who touted York's achievement. His article would be picked up by the press and, with America hungry for a war hero, York would return home to a hero's welcome, marry his sweetheart, Gracie, have a home built for him, a school named for him, a film made of his exploits, and spend the rest of his life being courted by the country's notables – and deservedly so. It should be noted that the press overlooked another soldier who was in York's company on that day and would survive 27 bullet holes and would receive the Distinguished Service Cross eight years later.

Calvin Ward's other awards would include Britain's Distinguished Conduct Medal, Belgium's War Cross, Portugal's War Cross third class, Italy's Croce di Guerra and Cross of Military Valor, France's Medaille Militaire and the Croix de Guerre with palm and tiny Montenegro's Medaille de Bravoure. While

York is frequently touted as the war's most decorated soldier, both Calvin Ward and Hamblen County's other Medal of Honor recipient, Edward Talley, would return home to far less recognition. That minimal recognition would continue to this day.

Calvin Ward, seventh from the left, second row, just after being presented with the Medal of Honor. (National Archives)

During the war, Calvin had written his father that he had been "over the top" three times and had come through without a scratch. His last letter would arrive on October 15th. His family had worried about his safety until hearing newspaper reports of his heroism.

Along with 3,000 men and officers, Calvin would board the transport ship Pocahontas on March 16, 1919, to come home. Morale officer L.J. Morse, along with two Y.M.C.A. men, would also come along to keep the soldiers entertained and contented throughout the long trip. A happy crowd would meet the ship at

Charleston, where several reporters had already heard about Calvin's achievement.

"Company D was being shot to pieces," Sergeant James E. 'Buck' Karnes would tell of Calvin's feat. "All of its officers had been put out of commission by wounds which incapacitated them for further action and the first-sergeant also, when Sergeant James E. Cox, acting first sergeant gave orders for Sergeant Karnes to take a platoon of men and rout out a machine gun nest. At the time the machine gun had up a deadly fire and was mowing down the Americans inflicting terrible casualties.

"Sergeant Karnes endeavored to do as ordered but found the ground impassable for several men. So, while the rest of the company kept up a terrific fire and kept the Germans attention centered on them Karnes and Ward crawled around the hill to the open spot where the machine guns were located and by a flank movement attacked. Ward jabbed the German officer in charge with his bayonet and the six other Huns were finished by bullets. The gun was thus captured. While this was being done, four other Germans were noticed in a menacing attitude and were fired upon. They were found to have been supporting a machine gun also."

On Saturday, April 5, 1919, the train carrying troops that included Calvin's unit would stop that morning in Morristown for the proud citizens to present the hero with a purse of money. The troops would then march in parades in Knoxville and Chattanooga. Calvin would receive his discharge on April 13th. While Edward Talley, who would have a home, wife and a business, would be more successful in readjusting, both men, and especially Calvin, would have difficulties in leaving the battlefield behind. In time, Calvin who in an early photo is shown to be an incredibly handsome young man, would become an almost forgotten hero.

While many combat veterans often return home to become the most solid and valued citizens and leaders, there are others who find it hard to escape the memories of their battlefield experiences. Their condition has had several names, including "shell shock," and currently has been renamed PTSD (Post Traumatic Stress Disorder). Some sufferers of the disorder would have to depend on alcohol to soften their memories. Calvin Ward would become one of those unfortunates.

Calvin Ward soon after he had returned home from World War I. (Cleo Sipe Purkey)

After returning to his mother's Morristown home, Calvin would find it difficult to adjust to civilian life and would re-enlist for a year in the Army's Sixth Cavalry's G Troop on November 5th, 1919. On November 18th, he would be admitted to the Ft. Oglethorpe hospital for acute bronchitis and would be found on the fort's census of January 3, 1920. He was listed as an illiterate but, because of his awards, was promoted to sergeant and exempted from all duties except for special classes. He would later be reduced in rank back to private because of inefficiency. Demons from the war, then not well understood, would haunt Ward. Bored and with time on his hands, he would drink heavily, become unruly and was often AWOL. He would soon begin missing classes and would gain a reputation as an unambitious and chronic drinker. After taking his awards into consideration, he would be quietly discharged on November 29th, 1920, at the end of his enlistment.

Enlisting again in the Sixth Cavalry's Supply Troop on December 7, 1920, he would again come under charges for drinking and being AWOL. On April 26, 1921, he would be discharged not honorably prior to the expiration of his term of enlistment, "on account of habits or traits of character which serve to render his retention in the service undesirable."

Determined to remain in the Army he would go to Richmond, Virginia, where on February 13th, 1923, he would enlist for three years in the 32nd Ordinance Company at Ft. Eustice, Virginia. He would claim no prior service at his enlistment, but upon being found out and because of his awards, would be allowed to remain. On Sunday night of May 27th, 1923, he would be charged with being drunk and disorderly in his quarters and

charged for assault when he hit another soldier in the arm with
his fist. This would subject him to a Summary Court Marshall
where he would be sentenced to hard labor and forfeiture of pay.
On November 7th, 1925, he would be charged with desertion and
would be discharged from the service by reason of desertion.
He would eventually become America's only Medal of Honor
recipient to receive an undesirable discharge.
uncharacterized

   The 1930 census would find Calvin at his Bristol, Virginia
home with his parents and two of his sisters, where his father
would be working as a night watchman at Sullins College. On
Sunday, February 1st, the Kingsport Times would report that "the
son is now in the government hospital, his mind occasionally
wandering." In that same article father Lewis would comment "If I
owned the whole world, I would gladly give a deed to it to have
my boy back as he once was."

   In November of 1930 he would be in Marion, Virginia's Davis
Clinic where he would be diagnosed with "Dementia Praecos"
(schizophrenia) and being "slightly mentally unbalanced", which
his doctor would state would possibly account for his desertion.
With his gassing during the war counting as a wound, he would
apply for a Purple Heart in 1937, but would be denied because of
inadequate records. A 1944 Bristol directory would again show
him living with his parents before leaving that year for painting
jobs along the Atlantic Coast. That would lead to work as an
automobile mechanic or a painter in such places as Baltimore
and Washington, D.C. On January 3, 1949, he would be charged
with drunkenness by the Bristol, Virginia police department.

Calvin Ward as he appeared c. 1930. (Cleo Sipe Purkey).

By May 4, 1950, he was in Bristol where he would marry Lucy Neal Lewis. The couple would separate in September when Ward would state that he was "Non Compos Mentis" (not of sound mind) and an Abstract of Divorce Degree dated April 22, 1957, would formally end the marriage through an annulment. Following another marriage, Lucy would pass away June 11, 1970, at age 64. During this stay in Bristol, Calvin would see a short period of peace when he joined the North Bristol Baptist Church but he would quit going when he felt out of place with the other members. It was while living in Bristol that all his medals were stolen from his home. It was also during this time that the Bristol office of the First National Exchange Bank of Virginia would begin managing his finances.

Calvin Ward with his mother Laura Ward (c.) and sisters Maxine, Mabel and Cleo. (Cleo Sipe Purkey).

Calvin Ward's house on Spurgeon Lane in Bristol. Members of his family would live there, while he would live there occasionally. (Cleo Sipe Purkey)

In the late 1950s Calvin would return to Morristown where he would stay at the old Morris Hotel, which sat just east of the later Kingmeyer Hotel. He was living in Morristown when on October 14th, 1961, he would write to get his Metal of Honor pension upped from $10 to $100 a month. This request would be granted and would become effective on October 31, 1961. In Morristown Calvin would become close to his namesake nephew, World War II Navy vet, Calvin Sipe, an expert auto restorer who had a shop that set across the street from today's Stetzer's Funeral Home. Adjacent to Sipe's shop was a shop operated by Chester Jobe, who was known as a master mechanic.

Never one to seek fame in memorials, print or gatherings, Ward was hospitalized out of state when his sister authorized his name being used when the Morristown Recreation Center name was changed to the Talley-Ward Recreation Center. Ward wouldn't object to his sister's authorization. Ward was again living in Bristol when he would hear of the passing of his now dear friend, Buck Karnes, who had died on July 8, 1966. Following that news, Calvin would suffer a breakdown resulting in his being taken to Mountain Home, leaving him unable to serve as a pallbearer for his friend.

Even after returning to Morristown, he was never able to recover from the emotional shock that would eventually end his life. While living at the Morris Hotel, Calvin would be with a friend when he put a .22 pistol to his heart and ended his life on December 15, 1967, at the age of 68. A Life Member of VFW Post 5266 he would be buried in Bristol's Glenwood Cemetery on December 17, 1967.

While a previous law only allowed Congressional Medal of Honor recipients with an honorable discharge to receive a government burial marker, Congressman Jimmy Quillen had pushed through a law that all MOH recipients, regardless of discharge, would receive a headstone. In a ceremony held at the cemetery on October 27, 1970, Calvin Ward would finally receive his marker.

Calvin would die an almost forgotten man in a run-down hotel room. Like so many others, he was unable to escape the ghosts of war.

References:

Claborn, Jim. "A Look Into The Life of Calvin J. Ward," *Morristown Citizen-Tribune, Morristown, TN. May 6, 1999.*

Claborn, Jim. "Who Was Calvin Ward?" Morristown Citizen-Tribune, Morristown, TN. May 25, 2014.

Department of Commerce and Labor, Bureau of the Census, "Thirteenth Census of the United States, 1910 Population," Hawkins County, Tennessee.

Department of Commerce, Bureau of the Census, "Fourteenth Census of the United States 1920 Population," Walker County Georgia.

Department of Commerce – Bureau of the Census, "Fifteenth Census of the United States 1930," Washington County, Virginia, Goodson District.

Hurley, Bob. *"Greene Native John Calvin Ward Was One of Four Most Decorated Doughboys,"* The Greeneville Sun, Greeneville, TN. May 8, 1976.

Hurley, Bob. *"Medal of Honor Winner Mostly Forgotten on The Dusty Road Where He Was Born,"* The Greeneville Sun, Greeneville, TN. May 23 1997.

Kingsport Times, *"Tennessee Forgets World War Heroes,"* Kingsport, Tennessee, Sunday, February 1, 1931.

Letter. The First National Exchange Bank of Virginia, Roanoke, Virginia. January 10, 1968.

Moore, William E. and Russell, James C. *"U.S. Official Pictures of the World War",* Distributed by Luckett Corporation, Chicago, Illinois, 1920.

Morristown Gazette. *"Morristown Boy Receives High Honors,"* Vol. LIII, No. 29, February 6, 1919.

Morristown Gazette. *"How Ward Won The Congressional Medal,"* No. 36, April 10, 1919.

National Personnel Record Center, St. Louis, Missouri.

Recap of the Estate of John Calvin Ward.

Chapter Six

REMEMBERING SERGEANT EDWARD ROBERT TALLEY

It's important to see a certified hero as a person, but Edward Talley's passing in 1950 makes it difficult to find anyone who knew him well. We were fortunate to have found three kinspersons who could draw an intimate picture of Edward Talley.

Mary Alice Harville

Mary Alice Moore Harville was the niece of Mattie Moore Talley and would stay with the Talleys for much of her young life. (Claborn)

Born in 1936, Mary Alice and her sister Ginger were the daughters of Fred and Ruth Evans Moore. Father Fred was the brother-in-law of Edward Talley. The family would soon move to Appalachia, Virginia where her father would work in the mines and later for Southern Railroad. In Appalachia they rented one of the rental houses owned by Edward and Mattie Moore Talley. The Talleys owned a line of rental houses as well as a large store where they lived in an upstairs apartment.

"We lived in one of the rental houses they had behind their grocery store and apartment, as well as beside the store and along the river," Mary Alice recalled. "I was with Aunt Mattie and Uncle Ed constantly and saw them daily. Uncle Ed was a big strong man who was gentle and kind, and was a well-versed butcher. It was in the '40s and he assigned me a job where I would go down the row houses and collect rent. It was something like $12 a month.

"Uncle Ed and Aunt Mattie had split homes. At the time they lived mostly in Appalachia but he had been born in Russellville and they had a home there that they'd built around 1936. Allen's Funeral Home is there today. After they had returned to Russellville he'd go back and forth to Appalachia in a big white van to haul produce like peaches and apples. Sometimes he'd also load the van with cases of eggs. He commuted sometimes once a week and one time my grandmother Moore and I were sitting in the back of the van in straight-back chairs when a bee from the fruit we were carrying went under her dress!

"After Uncle Ed and Aunt Mattie had moved back here he built a duplicate store across the street from their house. He was mainly a butcher and raised hogs and had Wiley Seals run the store. He also raised barley, oats and wheat, and shared threshing hands with the other local families like the Kings, Murrells and Carters. Uncle Ed was business smart in buying things at the right time, but Aunt Mattie drew the lines in the sand. She went to the First Baptist Church and was in church all the time. I always felt kind of tight around her, but loose around Uncle Ed. He was street-smart and not a dumb bunny by any means.

"We had also moved back and were living in Whitesburg. I wanted to go to Morristown High School and moved in with Uncle Ed and Aunt Mattie. He was a kind and gentle soul and she kept the books. They complemented each other and in my time I never heard them have a cross word. It's a shame that they didn't have any children because he was nurturing with children and loved all the nieces and nephews. He always had a meal in his truck and we had a lot of picnics and traveling. He would roll up his pants legs and wade in a creek with us.

"He'd stand by the window and wait for the school bus and I'd take my lunch and go to Jaybird Road to catch it. We always had family time in the sun room and would listen to Henry Aldridge and Lum and Abner. There was a large picture of him in his military uniform on a wall, with a medal near it, but he never talked at all about the war. I knew that he was a hero, but that was about all."

Judge James Edward "Eddie" Beckner

Judge James Edward "Eddie" Beckner was a great-nephew of Edward Talley and was his namesake. Eddie would spend many happy days with his "Uncle Ed."(Beckner)

In an effort to trace Sergeant Talley's footsteps, military historian Mike Beck, VFW historian Doyle Smith, Paul Murr, Jim Claborn and Hawkins County historian Donahue Bible made a trip to Appalachia, Virginia, where Edward and Mattie had moved following his return from the war. Their former store, which bears a small plaque noting Sergeant Talley's achievement, still stands alongside the river, as do several of their formal rental homes. Eddie Beckner is one of the three children of Morristown native Olen Beckner and Iantha Hopkins Beckner. He was born in Appalachia, where he would begin his education at Appalachia School. During Eddie's younger years, he would spend much time with his great-uncle.

"My mother gave me the name James after her brother who had died and Edward after Uncle Ed," he told. "He would kid me and say 'You were named after me and you're going to have to shape up!' I was 11 and a-half years old when he died. He and his wife Mattie didn't have any children so they were very close to Mary Alice and me. My mother told me that he bought me my first stroller and snowsuit. We rented a house from him for four years and rented the store from him for nine years, where we lived in the apartment over the store.

"He was a kind and gentle person and was a comfort and a joy to be around. Uncle Ed would come and see me and give me a silver dollar every time he came, and would give me several on my birthdays. I had about 60 silver dollars when a carnival came to town. My parents had forbidden me to go but I loaded my pockets with silver dollars and went anyway. I spent a few of them on rides and the rest of them throwing balls, until they finally gave me a Mother's Day pin that I wanted. Daddy put the rest of them where I couldn't get them and spanked me – which he should have.

"Uncle Ed would often take me on trips to town and to High Knob to ride around. I remember talking about what he did in the war. The way he expressed it was that the Lord was looking after what he did and that he wasn't a hero. He told that they were in an open area when the event occurred and that they were like sitting ducks and were trying to find cover. One friend right close to him had been hit and he picked up the man's dog tags and went charging right into two machine gun positions. When he wiped one machine gun out, he used the gun to quieten the other one down.

"When we would come down to Russellville from Appalachia, we would go fishing on Cherokee Lake near the Hamblen Boat

Dock and he would fry walleye for breakfast. It was a long trip from Appalachia over rough roads. He had a 66 acre farm in Russellville with a Black Heart cherry orchard and was happiest when he was farming and raising hogs. He was a good butcher and loved doing it. He had a great respect for the flag and would tell that the red stood for blood, the white for purity and the blue for beauty.

"My family had been renting the store in Appalachia and we were struggling because the miners had been on their second long strike. The store was going down the drain because Daddy had been giving the miners credit and the wholesalers wouldn't give us credit. Daddy sold everything he owned to pay the wholesalers and got a job with Southern railroad in Bulls Gap and after living for a while in Gilley's Hotel, we moved to Morristown."

Bill Moore

Bill Moore at Edward Talley's gravesite in Whitesburg. (Claborn)

Originally from Whitesburg and 78 years-old at this writing, Bill Moore is another of Mattie Moore Talley's nephews who still has vivid memories of his "Uncle Ed."

"I can remember Uncle Ed since I was six or seven years old," he started. "Ed and Mattie didn't have any children and my brother Curtis and sister Verda and I used to come stay with them for a while. We didn't have an indoor toilet and they did. The first time we flushed their toilet, it scared us! Aunt Mattie was very finicky about things and would take us one at a time to spend the weekend with them at Appalachia. They soon moved to their home in Russellville where the funeral home is today.

"Aunt Mattie was close with her money and would give us nickels and dimes and would let us get a bar of candy occasionally. Uncle Ed was friendly and a joker and he'd out-give her and would give us nieces and nephews 50 cents at a time. When they lived in Russellville, he had the store across the road and would take us into his section of the store to get what we wanted. They never had any children of their own and he took care of us kids and would take us for rides in his car.   He would never mention the war at all. He had a farm at Russellville and loved to work on it. Somebody would run his store full time and Wylie Seals run it there at the last. We've still got a magazine rack and a couple of pillows from their home and my sons got his old .22 rifle.

"When he was young, Ed had worked in the mines and on the railroad from Rockwood to Danville. When they were going to present him the medal they communicated with him to come to Washington, D.C., but he told them that if they wanted him to have it to bring it to him, and they did. There was an all-day celebration when he got his medal at the First Baptist Church at Whitesburg. When he got sick there at the last, he wouldn't go to the hospital until the last minute. I was 12 years old when they had his funeral at the cemetery and remember that they gave him a 21-gun salute."

Chapter Seven

MEMORIES OF PRIVATE CALVIN JOHN WARD

Maxine Meade

Michael Beck with Maxine Meade, who would be Calvin Ward's last surviving sister. (Claborn)

Having begun a study of Calvin Ward in the 1990s the chances of finding someone with an intimate knowledge of Ward appeared grim. It was then that former Rose Center director Bill Kornrich mentioned to military historian Mike Beck that Ward still had a sister living in Bristol, Virginia. Mike began a telephone relationship with that sister, Maxine Meade, and would call to tell that she would be happy to see us. It was a beautiful Sunday when a lively and stylish Maxine met us at her door to begin a pleasant evening of looking over photos, documents and the family Bible. Our visit with Maxine would finally give us an idea of Calvin as he was as a person.

From Maxine we learned that Calvin was the only son of Alvin and Laura Ward's eight children. She would tell that her brother had been born in his grandfather's hilltop log cabin at Guthrie's Gap, near Tennessee's Hawkins and Greene County borders. By 1915 the Wards were living in Morristown, Tennessee. On July 14, 1917, Calvin joined the National Guard and listed his home with his mother at 748 First North Street, Morristown, Tennessee.

"When he went in, the doctor couldn't find his pulse," Maxine told. "He let him peck around a little and then told him about his heart being on the other side. Following the war, and with his family moving to Bristol, Calvin liked to often return to Morristown because he liked to go to our sister Essie's house because she was a good cook.

"During the war he was gassed and shell-shocked and that did affect his mind. He told me that the helmet he wore was shot to pieces and his overcoat was hanging by strings, but he never got a bullet in him. He as just a plain soldier, but I do think he had a right rough time in service. He picked up a little bit of French. One time a man said 'Bon Chez, Monsieur' and he wanted to fight him because he thought the man was calling him 'barnyard manure.'

"Nobody knows the home life we had. The government bought him a house on Spurgeon Lane in Bristol, but he never come around much and never seemed satisfied. When he'd get his check, he'd go to town and come in without any money. He'd borrow money from me, but he'd always pay it back.

"My mother tried to keep him straight. She said that he was a good child who never gave her any trouble and that before the service he had never had a drink of liquor. He comes back a drunkard. When a car load of men would come by to get him, she would run them off. He said that when he was in the service that he always wanted a good drink of water. Calvin did have a year of peace when he joined the North Bristol Baptist Church, but he quit after a year because 'wouldn't anybody have nothing to do with me.'"

Maxine also told that Calvin would often go to the nearby veterans' hospital in Johnson City. The hospital once told the rowdy Ward that the next time he came in he had better be on a stretcher.

"He'd seem to get a little better, but would soon go to town and get drunk" she said. "I'd always try to get up and let him in before he woke up our mother. He once came in and tried to light a cigarette on a light bulb. My mother would often hide his shotgun. When Mother and Dad died, he told us that he wanted us to stay. The next week he went to town and come back dog drunk, bawling us out. We lived in that house a long time before it burned."

Maxine was quick to recall the more pleasant times with her brother.

"He loved kids. He'd pick them up and show them his dogs. He was a painter and went to Baltimore and painted a lot. He told me that a good painter never spilled any paint and doesn't go the same way with a brush all the time.

"Calvin never sought publicity. He was invited to many distinguished gatherings but never went. The name of the Talley-Ward Recreation Center was authorized by a sister because he was hospitalized in another state, but he didn't object."

In a 1997 column in the Greeneville Sun, writer Bob Hurley would add another telling comment from Maxine:

"Mother said that when the troop train brought Calvin back, he held me in his arms. The whole community was there to brag and wave at him. Mother said that he looked so fine and good looking."

Donahue Bible

Donahue Bible near the Calvin Ward birthsite at Guthrie's Gap in Hawkins County shows Paul "Eddie" Murr and Mike Beck some World War I artifacts. (Claborn)

Donahue Bible is a very knowledgeable historian about the Greene/Hawkins/Hamblen County areas and had also been friends with Calvin Sipe, Ward's nephew and namesake. Donahue recalled Sipe's story of a lady magazine writer from out of town who stopped by Sipe's and Chester Jobe's Morristown Main Street garage and body shop. She was looking for information on how to contact Ward for an article that she was intending to write.

"Ward liked to visit with his nephew, Calvin Sipe, and he liked to be left alone," Donahue told. "Calvin Ward just happened to be in an adjoining room during the lady's visit and heard her request. He reluctantly came out of the room to announce 'Lady, if you want to know about the Army, join up and find out for yourself.' That ended her chance for an interview."

Dr. Caleb "Bud" Jones

Longtime Morristown pharmacist, Caleb "Bud" Jones would recall Calvin coming into Morristown's Freels Drug Store, where Jones worked at the time. (Claborn)

"Morristown didn't have legal beer at the time," Jones told. "Calvin lived in the hotel and would eat downtown and would hang out at Speck's Pool Room. He was a small man about 5' 7" or 5' 8", with a medium build and with nothing outstanding about his physical appearance and was sort of quiet. He had an alcohol problem, but never appeared drunk. He got a Dorian pill every day that would work against alcohol, but I never seen him under the influence. He never done anything to call attention to himself and was never obnoxious and it was easy to ignore him. He was a nondescript dresser, but after he got an extra bonus there was a physical change because he had the money to dress better. I think that Claude Rogers made sure that he got well-fitting clothing. It's long about (sic) time that something was named for him."

Cleo Sipe Purkey

As we were searching for someone with a lengthy recall of Calvin Ward, Bill Keeny would call to announce, "If you want to learn about Calvin Ward, why don't you just call his niece, Cleo Sipe Purkey?"

With that good news, I called Mrs. Purkey, who graciously agreed to visit with myself and Mike Beck. Then 85, Mrs. Purkey, a longtime Morristown resident, would soon be into an interesting story about her beloved uncle.

The daughter of Walter "Pappy" Sipe, who had run the Hamblen County Boat Dock, and Essie Ward Sipe, Cleo was raised on Morristown's Daisy Street along with siblings Helen, Joie, Earnest, Bill, Calvin (Calvin Ward's namesake) and Bearl. As a youngster, she had attended Rose School and Morristown

Junior High School. In 1947 she would marry Dick Purkey, a truck driver and World War II vet who had served as a sergeant in the European Theater, where he had earned the Purple Heart. Her brother Calvin had joined the Navy at 17, had helped clean up Hiroshima, and would remain close to his decorated uncle. Following the war, Calvin Sipe, along with Chester Jobe would run a popular Main Street garage.

Cleo Sipe Purkey would be Calvin's last living niece and would have many memories of her uncle. (Claborn)

Cleo shared her memories of her uncle.

"Calvin's dad, Lewis, was a good old man who worked at King's College," she started. "His mother was a good woman as well. They're both buried at Bristol. Calvin's sisters were Essie, Nola, Cleo, Mary, Maxine and another who died young. After they left Greene County, they moved here, first out Valley Home Road, then to a big two-story house on the Corner of Second

North and High Street. There's a law office there now. Mama was a little girl when they lived at Bull's Gap.

"I was ten years old when we moved here on Daisy Street. Our family was always proud of him. He was a good and decent man who wasn't loud and didn't cuss and carry on and wouldn't joke much. He never changed much and always looked the same. He was a loner and wasn't very sociable and was very private and didn't hardly have any friends. He never talked about the war at all. My oldest sister was an old maid and had some pictures of him, but I don't know what happened to them after she died.

"Mama just thought that he was the stuff and was closer to him than the rest. He would always come and see Mama because she wouldn't fuss at him and would cook for him, but he would never stay all night because he always stayed at the old hotel down below the Kingmeyer. He always dressed up and never went slouchy. He liked to hang out at Roddy's Pool Room on Henry Street and I never did know him to work. He was always kind to me.

"Calvin owned a nice two-story home on Spurgeon's Lane in Bristol that the government gave him. He let his family live there and he lived there when he was around. I don't know if they sold the house or what happened to it. I think I remember that it caught on fire. Calvin didn't like women and didn't have any girlfriends, but I think that he was married to someone in Bristol for a while. He used to go to Bristol to visit, but in his last years he lived here more.

"People just accepted Calvin the way he was. When he wasn't drinking, he was miserable. He got drunk and done away with a lot of his medals, but they got some of them back. When he died, he was ready to go. He could have had it all, but he didn't want it."

Bill Henderson

As a young boy Bill Henderson would spend time around Morristown's downtown, where he would get to know Calvin Ward. (Claborn)

Bill is the premier historian of the area and is a man blessed with a remarkable memory that goes back to his Morristown childhood. As a 12 or 13 year-old boy, Bill got to know Calvin Ward.

"He had a round face, was dark-headed and wore flannel shirts and corduroy pants. He spent a lot of time sleeping upstairs on Main Street in the hall between the barber shop and Frank Davis' office. Calvin had a bag to sleep in and nobody bothered him. Every once in a while Frank Davis or Billy Lampkin would get him a room and I've seen Frank Lorino give him meals at the back of the Little Dutch Restaurant.

"I'd see him sitting on the steps of those stairs going up to Frank Davis' office and would talk to him. He'd wave at us. I've never seen him drunk. He was no panhandler and had pride, but I'd give him a nickel or dime every once in a while and sometimes he'd give me something. He was good to all us kids. I'd also see him sitting on the bench at the Jud Matthews or Nick Matthews store. He was sort of a loner. I'd rack balls at Roddy's pool room and he'd spend a lot of time there. He'd be sitting there in a chair. He was quiet and wore regular clothes. He had been AWOL in the Army before going overseas and instead of charging him, they put him on the boat and sent him to the front lines with hardly any training.

"I asked him about the Medal of Honor and he said 'Billy, they just made me into a hero. I was still sick when the Germans pushed us out of our camp and pushed us back four or five hundred yards and they were eating our food. Our orders were not to attack before we got reinforcements. The sun was up and them boys were making fun of us and enjoying our stuff. I said that it's either them or me and them boys grabbed their guns and they'd jump up.' I think that all that killing was weighing on him."

References:

Claborn, Jim. "A Look Into The Life of Calvin J. Ward?," *Morristown Citizen-Tribune*, Morristown, TN., May 6, 1999.

Claborn, Jim. "Who Was Calvin Ward?" *Morristown Citizen-Tribune*, Morristown, TN. May 25, 2014.

Hurley, Bob. "Pvt. Calvin John Ward Won More Medals than Sgt. Alvin C. York, But He Is Mostly Forgotten," *The Greeneville Sun*, Greeneville, TN, Volume 118, Number 155, Friday, May 23, 1997.

Hurley, Bob. "Medal of Honor Winner Mostly Forgotten On The Dusty Road Where He Was Born," *The Greeneville Sun*, Greeneville, TN. May 23, 1997.

Chapter Eight

COMING HOME

Welcome Home poster in Knoxville Sentinel, March 29, 1919.

Following the terrible fighting around the Selle River, the 30th Division would be relieved and would move to the Tincour-Brouely area where it would remain through October 22nd. On October 23rd the Division would move to the Querrieu area where it would undergo rehabilitation and was expecting an order to be returned to the front. On Sunday, November 10, 1918, an armistice to end the war was signed to cease all hostilities at 11:00 a.m. the next morning.

Allied commanders across the front lines would direct that attacks be continued against the enemy until the moment of the cease fire. Those orders would cause the death of almost 3,000 Americans, more than would be killed on D-Day on June 6, 1944. At one minute before 11:00, Sergeant Henry Gunther of Baltimore, Maryland would be struck by a bullet and killed just before the battlefield quietened. He would be the last American to die during World War I.

A moment later, soldiers would begin to realize that they had survived the war. Like any soldier of any war, the foremost thought on the minds of most soldiers would be going back home. However, for most of the American doughboys, that wait would last for several very long months. With peace at hand, the commanders would soon find that they had the new problem of containing 2,000,000 excited and homesick soldiers.

Morristown crowds gather at the Canteen to celebrate the Armistice. (Morristown Red Cross)

That problem would be approached by assigning soldiers to work details, more hours of drilling, ceremonial formations and marches, recreation and sporting events, and train trips to Paris. For most of the men of the 30th Division, the long wait to return home would end in March, 1919.

On November 16th the 30th Division had been taken out of Allied control and placed back under the umbrella of the American Expeditionary Force. Three days later, and still without their artillery brigade, the 30th would move to the American Embarcation Center at LeMans, where they would be rejoined by their artillery brigade in early February. The Division would remain in camp in the LeMans area and would not be a part of the Army of Occupation. On February 18th the Trench Mortar Battery would sail from Brest for the United States. On March 4th the remainder of the Division would move to the area of the harbor at St. Naizaire, where they would begin their trip home on March 6th.

At 2:00 p.m. on March 16, 1919, 78 officers and 2,841 men who were almost all members of the 30th Division, as well as one Y.M.C.A. civilian, would board the transport U.S.S. Pocahontas at St. Nazaire to return to the United States. The 117th and 118th Infantry Regiments had made up most of the cargo with 50 officers and 2,027 men being of the 117th Regiment commanded by Colonel Gary F. Spence, and 27 officers and 971 men of the 118th Regiment. Other units on the Pocahontas would include Headquarters and staff, Headquarters of the First battalion, the Ordinance detachment and Companies A to F inclusive. On March 20th the ship would pass the Azores Islands. During the trip a mild epidemic of influenza would develop, with 34 cases reported. Private Edward H. King of Co. L, 118th Regiment would be the epidemic's only fatality and would die just after the ship had anchored back in the United States.

The U.S.S. Pocahontas would return the men of the 117th Infantry Regiment back home to the U.S. in March, 1919. (National Archives)

At 6:15 p.m. on March 27, 1919, the ship would be anchored off Ft. Sumter, South Carolina and would dock at North Charleston at 11:06 a.m. on the 28th. There the troops, along with those on the Koningin Der Nederlanden, would be debarked immediately at the port terminals. Both ships had arrived the day before. The men who had landed at Charleston then proceeded to Camp Jackson for final delousing and new uniforms. Awaiting them were special trains used to carry them to Camp Jackson to hasten demobilization with the final sections leaving in the early afternoon. The remaining elements of the 30th

Division would arrive at Charleston on April 18th. With politicians and the local public wanting to see and welcome the soldiers back home, several parades were planned before the remaining men could get their final discharges at Fort Oglethorpe, Georgia.

Throughout the war the local citizens had shown strong support for the war, with one prime example being the Red Cross Canteen in Morristown. With the difficulties and congestion of transporting millions of soldiers making it impossible for soldiers to receive adequate meals during their trips, the United States government made a request of the American Red Cross. That request would be that the Red Cross provide refreshments for the troop trains at important junctions both in-country and abroad.

As a result of that request, the Red Cross Canteen Service was founded and would grow quickly. By the end of 1917 there would be 85 canteen depots, 15 station restaurants and 430 smaller units that would be staffed by 55,000 mostly women volunteers. Of those canteens, the one in Morristown would receive rave reviews from service members from across the country.

In a letter home dated August 11, 1918, Will Murrell would make mention of the Morristown Canteen. Murrell, the son of Rev. M.M. Murrell of early airplane fame, would become a long-serving Morristown educator. In his letter he would comment that "I am certainly proud of Morristown's Canteen. It must be the best in the whole country. Anyway, it is the best that I have ever heard of. The best treatment that we got on our way down here was at Rome, Ga. They gave us all the Coco-Cola (sic) and Chero-Cola that we could drink. At Knoxville they gave each boy a cigarette and a postcard. Nowhere have I heard of the Canteens serving square meals except at Morristown. The sergeant here, a good friend of mine from Ohio, tells me that the Southern people treat the soldiers much better than the Northern people."

These women were several of the many volunteers of the Morristown Chapter of the Red Cross which would provide food drinks and other comforts to the men and women coming through on troop trains. Pictured (l.to r. seated) are unknown, Mrs. Lewis Noe, Lucille Pullen, (standing) Mrs. J.B. Christmas, Ms. Akers, Mrs. Drinnon, unknown, unknown, Irene Willis, unknown. (Morristown Red Cross)

In a letter to the Morristown Red Cross Canteen from Camp Merrit, New Jersey dated August 29, 1918, John W. Davis, Jr. would write, "We arrived at our destination safely, and will leave for overseas soon. It has been the talk among the boys of how well the Morristown people treated them. I am sure the whole train will vouch for me in saying that Morristown cared for us as well or better than the large cities such as Washington, Baltimore Philadelphia and other eastern towns, which of course, made me very proud of Hamblen County."

Booth set up on Morristown's Main Street to sell Liberty Bonds to passersby while "Uncle Am" Stuart played his fiddle. Pictured are Stuart and volunteers Mary Hodge Dosser and Olive "Ollie" Rogers. (Rose Center)

Articles in the local newspaper would continue to mention individually the hundreds of citizens who had contributed to the canteen. Donations for the local canteen would also come in from the surrounding counties and from as far as Walnut Creek, North Carolina. Also noted was that while W.E. Mullins had served as the County Canteen Chairman and Lynn Sheely as the Publicity Chairman, eight-tenths of the work had been done by the good ladies of the area.

One article would also add "Let us right here thank our good neighbors, Greene County, Cocke County, Jefferson County, Grainger County, and Hawkins County for their much appreciated gifts during the life of our Canteen, more especially during the last few weeks."

On October 19, 1918, a proud Hamblen County Red Cross Canteen would post, "Our Canteen is famous. It is referred to in every part of the United States and even in France, as one of the best organized and most efficient Canteens ever operated by any county. We are doubly sure that no county the size of Hamblen in the United States has anything in the line of a Canteen to compare with it."

Shortly after the war a soldier who had been served at the canteen would write to then Canteen Chairman Sullins Dosser, "Dear Folks: Just a few lines to let you and your co-workers know how very much we appreciated the wonderful treatment we received at your hands as we passed thru Morristown Saturday a week ago. Those plate lunches were delightful and it was marvelous the way you folks got them distributed in five minutes time.

"I spent nineteen months in France and visited many live Red Cross Canteens but when it comes to efficient organization yours gets the palm, while nothing in the world can beat 'Southern Eats'.

"My home is in Mississippi, but you Tennessee people have shown us all such a wonderful reception that part of my heart will always be in Tennessee. Morristown may be 'a little town', but I know it has 'A big welcome', so big in fact that the name will always look large on the map to me.

"Assuring you again how much we appreciated your gracious hospitality, and with all good wishes for your Red Cross Chapter, I am. Very sincerely yours, F.S. HARMON, 2nd Lieut. 114th F.A."

By October, 1918, the Canteen averaged 319 service men per day. After seven months, 102,603 servicemen had been served. By February 6, 1919, it was noted that workers carried hot meals onto the train to serve the wounded. These men usually traveled in special coaches.

With the soldiers so eager to get home, six trains on the Southern and L & N Railways would be held up briefly. Approximately 4000 out of town visitors would arrive in Knoxville on Friday evening and Saturday morning to take part in the reception. Southern and L & N had also scheduled special trains to bring in visitors for the event. Local Morristown captains would awaken their workers at 2:30 a.m. on Friday, April 4, 1919, for a special morning. At 4:30 a.m. the town would be awakened by a shrill whistle signaling that their heroes of the 117th Infantry would be arriving within a half hour. As dawn broke welcome banners surrounded by ropes of lights, rows of trucks decorated with flowers, and trays of food prepared by happy workers in their uniforms with waving veils would be waiting for the train.

The first train would arrive at 5 a.m. sharp and would be welcomed by the whistles of four nearby huge engines. A mob of people from around the area would immediately surround the train making it difficult for Colonel Spence to tell of his appreciation for Morristown's welcome to his boys. Five other trains would arrive at half-hour intervals to be served 3,000 delicious meals by the Morristown Canteen.

Calvin Ward had arrived on the first train and was allowed to stay in the city until the last train would take him onward. At 7:00 a.m. Mayor Donaldson would step on a truck with Ward and make an appropriate talk of Ward's bravery and express the area's pride in his heroism. He would then present Ward with a new $100 bill which had been donated by citizens. Ward would then turn and present the money to his mother, which brought applause from the crowd. The soldiers of the 117th were high in their praises to Morristown and the generous people who had donated and prepared the feast that was fed to 3,000 men in just five hours.

Demobilization of the 117th would begin on April 13th with Companies A through D being given their discharge papers, while Companies E through H would be sent home the next day (Tuesday). Companies I, K, L and M would leave on Wednesday, while Thursday was set for the departure for the Headquarters unit. Calvin Ward and Edward Talley would soon return home to begin the rest of their lives.

Upon their discharge, soldiers were told that they could "keep all their cooties". Along with their pay enlisted men who had served overseas could keep a shirt, service coat, a pair of shoes, leggings and britches, as well as their gas mask, helmet an barracks bag. Colonel Carey F. Spence, the commanding officer, would issue a general order to all the men expressing his regret at parting with his heroic followers who had fought together "on the stricken fields of France".

On April 29th, the Greeneville Daily Sun would post an article from the proud Colonel Spence telling that the East Tennesseans of the 117th were a tall lot. "Exactly 594 of the men of the 117th regiment, composed mostly of East Tennesseans were over six feet tall and one man was six feet and seven inches in height. They (the men of the 117th) were mostly from the East Tennessee mountains and were second only to the fearless Australians as intrepid fighters," he told. Spence also noted his men's huge appetites. "The men could clean out a canteen in no time and when the mess call was sounded go at it again as if they'd had nothing to eat since they came over.

For the citizens of Morristown another reminder of the war would be the "Victory Tank", which would arrive by rail on April 30th to be displayed to the local citizens. Still carrying the scars of the Argonne and St. Mihiel battles, the tank was an American machine which had been used in the closing months of the war. Taken from the railroad flatcar, the tank was exhibited on the corner of Henry and Main Streets. There several interesting talks were given on the performance of the tank, several of which were made by accompanying veterans who had served on tanks. The tank had stopped at Corryton and Rutledge that morning and was scheduled to be in Jefferson City, Newport and Dandridge in the coming days.

Local citizens were eager to see an actual World War I combat tank when the "Victory Tank" traveled through Morristown following the war. (Red Cross)

By late spring, and with most of the soldiers back home, Chairman Sullins Dosser would call a meeting of the Canteen workers to discuss how much longer the Canteen should remain open. The majority at the meeting would favor keeping the Canteen open until July 15th. At the meeting, captains of the Wednesday and Thursday teams, Mrs. George Donaldson and Mrs. Sam Willis would tender their resignations and would be replaced by Mrs. Fred Davis and Mrs. George Portrum. Because of work and declining health, Mr. Dosser would also tender his resignation and would be replaced by "Uncle Am" Stuart. A well-known fiddle player, Uncle Am had been one of the Canteen's most devoted supporters.

The summer of 1919 would see the country begin to leave the thoughts of wartime and begin to look toward a brighter future. The near future, however, would be filled with the ending of the terrible pandemic of the influenza outbreak before the country could enjoy "The Roaring Twenties". That decade would be followed by ten years of hard times during the Great Depression, and the coming of the most horrible war that the world has ever experienced, World War II. For Edward Talley and Calvin Ward, World War I would follow them though out their lives.

References:

American Red Cross Hamblen County Chapter 1917 – 1980. George S. Hale, Jr.

Boland, Micajai, U.SS. Pocahontas Ship's Log, "A History of the War Activities of U.S.S. Pocahontas", European War pamphlets, Volume 59, 1919.

Browe, Amanda, American Red Cross, Red Cross Chat, "From the Archives, Women of the Canteen Service, March 6, 2014.

Greeneville Daily Sun, "East Tennesseans in 117th Infantry Were a Tall Lot", April 29, 1919.

Knoxville News Sentinel, "Welcome Home" poster, March 29, 1919.

Morristown Evening Mail, "Prof. Will Murrell Writes Very Interesting Letter Home" and "Appreciation of Red Cross Canteen," September 3, 1918

Morristown Evening Mail, "Hamblen County Red Cross Canteen Most Efficient", "Contributions To R.C. Canteen", "Donations to Red Cross Canteen," October 19, 1918.

Morristown Evening Mail, "Demobilization of the 117th Begins", April 14, 1919.

Morristown Evening Mail, "117th Heroes Welcomed", April 16, 1919.

Morristown Evening Mail, "Tank Here-Veteran of St. Mihiel and Argonne Forest Battles Seen Today", April 30, 1919.

Morristown Evening Mail, "Many Visitors to See 117th", "Mississippi Boy Writes Canteen Workers", "Canteen Will Remain Open Till July 15th", undated clippings, 1919.

U.S. Army Center of Military History, "Order of Battle of the United States Land Forces in the World War, 1917-1919", 1988, first printed 1931.

30th Division, "Summary of Operations in the World War" prepared by the American Battle Monuments Commission created by Congress in 1923.

Chapter Nine

PHOTOS

(American Troops Arriving in France) By 1918, thousands of American troops would be arriving in France weekly to be welcomed by the exhausted Allied forces. (National Library of Scotland)

Clarence Blevins of Russellville, shown with his sister Mrs. Essie Bristol, would be one of nearly 500 Hamblen County men called to service in World War I. Mrs. Bristol would be a longtime teacher in the Greene and Hawkins County school systems. (Claborn/Henderson)

American troops arriving at Templeaux on September 28,1918, to join the Australians in the attack on the Hindenburg Line. (Australian War Memorial)

American troops watching the 3rd Australian Division passing through the streets of a village on October 14, 1918, on their way to the fighting beyond the village. American and Australian units would fight alongside each other in the breaking of the Hindenburg Line. (Australian War Memorial)

When ordered "over the top" Allied soldiers would often have to cross such wire entanglements on an attack on the Hindenburg Line. (National Library of Scotland)

Two unidentified American soldiers atop a Mark V tank that was stopped by a ditch in the Hindenburg Line. (Australian War Memorial)

Enterprising troops found a secondary use for tanks by using them to carry supplies over uneven and dangerous ground. (National Archives)

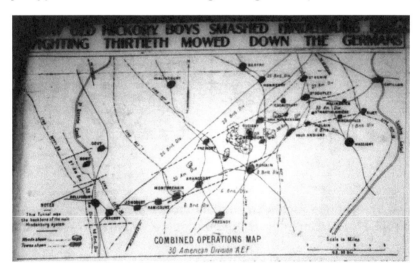

This map shows much of the French area that was fought over by the 30th Infantry Division. (The Nashville Tennessean)

Members of Company K, 117th Regiment, 30th Infantry Division digging themselves in for the night on October 17, 1918, for an advance on Molain, France the following morning. (National Archives)

Allied warplane flying over France. (Charlie Buchanan, WWI soldier)

Dismantling Austrian 380mm Skoda gun left at Dannevoux. (Charlie Buchanan, WWI soldier)

Edward and Mattie Talley at their Russellville home c. 1950. (Bill Moore)

Photo of Calvin Ward taken c. 1944 most likely at Bristol where he participated in World War II bond drives. (Citizen-Tribune)

Memorial placed by the Morningside Garden Club in 1932 commemorating the Hamblen County soldiers who died in World War I. The memorial lists (Army) Sgt. Tip M. Allen, Pvt. William Blackwell, 2nd Lt. William Bushowg (Bushong?), Pvt. James Cantwell, Pvt. Donald Eugene Cardwell, Pvt. Alonzo Carter, Pvt. William Carter, Pvt. Bruce M. Colboch, Pvt. Simon Cole, Pvt. Marcus M. Dellas, ASN Odp Eses Pvt Grady Harris, PFC Charles E. Smith, Sgt. James M. West, (Navy) Appr. Seaman George Robert Donaldson and Appr. Seaman John Stuart Good. (Underwood)

INDEX

France, Bellicourt, 30, 33, 34, 36, 37, 46

G

L

L& N Railway, 113
Lampkin, Billy, 102
Lankhof Farm, 28
Lewis, Lucy Neal, 81
Lewis, MG Edward M., 20, 29, 60
Liberty Bonds, 111
Lillard, Cpt. David, 53, 58, 59*ph*, 68
Little Dutch Restaurant, 102
Lock No. 8, 28
London Double-decker buses, 39
Lorino, Frank, 102
Lum and Abner, 88
Lusitania, 36
Lynn Sheely Company, 12

M

Malakoff Farm, 30
Mark V tank, 33, 124*ph*
Marne, Battle of
Mary the Elephant, 11
Matthews Store, 103
Medal of Honor, 1-8, 18, 52, 54, 58, 61-62*ph*-64, 66, 68, 70, 73-76, 80, 83
Meuse-Argonne Offensive, 73
Mexican Punitive Expedition, 20
Mexican-American War, 19
Mexico, 13, 19
Militia Company of East Tennessee, 19
MILLS 23 grenades, 32
Mississippi, 113
Mohawk, TN, 71